GOLF

About the authors

Few persons could be better qualified to write about learning the grand game of golf than Virginia L. Nance (Mrs. Edward K.). She has participated in all levels of competition, from a youngster in local and junior events to the major amateur women's tournaments, including the U.S. Amateur for Women. She has been medalist, semifinalist, runner-up, and winner of many tournaments.

But Mrs. Nance has excelled even more as a teacher, giving both private and class lessons to boys and girls, men and women, in high schools, at golf-practice ranges, in camps, and at colleges and universities. She has conducted numerous golf clinics for students and teachers at local, state, and national levels. Mrs. Nance is a Class A Teaching Member of the Ladies Professional Golf Association. She has been a contributor of articles for DGWS and AAHPER publications. She holds degrees from the University of Illinois and the University of Wisconsin and has completed further graduate work at the University of Southern California.

Mrs. Nance's coauthor, Dr. Elwood Craig Davis, is a well-known and distinguished professor of physical education, having been associated with major institutions such as Pennsylvania State University, University of Pittsburgh, University of Louisville, University of Southern California. He is presently with California State University at Northridge. He has enlivened summer sessions at the University of Washington, University of Oregon, and Utah State University. His honors are legion, the most outstanding perhaps being a recipient of the Phi Epsilon Kappa National Award and both the American Academy of Physical Education's Hetherington Award and the AAAPER's Luther Halsey Gulick Medal.

Dr. Davis is a graduate of the University of Washington, University of Chicago, and Columbia University. Service was in U.S. Naval Aviation and Naval Physical Training. He is the author or coauthor of nine books and numerous articles.

GOLF

Physical Education Activities Series

Virginia Lindblad Nance

Class A Teaching Member
Ladies Professional Golf Association
Formerly, University of Southern California

Elwood Craig Davis

California State University at Northridge
Emeritus, University of Southern California

Illustrations by Francile Otto and Ralph Rivas

THIRD EDITION

Wm C Brown Company Publishers
Dubuque, Iowa

Consulting Editor

Aileene Lockhart
Texas Woman's University

Evaluation Materials Editor

Jane A. Mott
Smith College

Copyright © 1966, 1971, 1975 by Wm. C. Brown Company Publishers

Library of Congress Catalog Card Number: 74-27900

ISBN 0—697—07062—X

Printed in the United States of America

Contents

Preface

This, the third edition of *Golf*, continues toward the same dual objectives as those established for previous editions: to present information that will enable the reader to become well-grounded in the knowledge of golf as a game; and to present the golf strokes in a simple but thorough way so that the reader may become a more intelligent and a more enlightened student of the game—better able to learn and develop skill in the strokes.

To accomplish the first objective, knowledge of the game, an entirely new feature has been added. At the end of the book the reader will find a 200-question test consisting of 140 true-false and 60 essay-type questions. Golf terms, etiquette, safety, and rules are covered in the test. The complaints circulating throughout the golfing world are to the effect that too many players either do not know how to conduct themselves on the course or they inconsiderately ignore the accepted traditional practices of the game. We have tackled this problem in previous editions, but this time we hope we have really "hit the nail on the head." In our opinion, this test is in the nature of a "driver's test," for all golfers. The odds are that even the experienced golfer will not make a perfect score on this one! In fact the golfer may be surprised to find that it will be necessary to refer to the rule book for some answers. The test may be modified for the inexperienced player—test items on match play, for example, may be postponed for later study. We have intentionally avoided making the test a simple one, because we feel that any real student wishes to gain a thorough knowledge of the accepted procedures and will want to uphold the fine traditions of golf. We recommend that you pass this test before you play your *first* game of golf or before you play your *next* round of golf.

Other sections have been expanded and updated. For example, certain procedures to speed up play on the course have become common practice today. Details of these have been added to the section on etiquette. Out of consideration for other people on the course and to rescue the novice from possible embarrassing situations resulting from lack of skill, we have recommended procedures that may lead some reader to think we advise players to ignore the rules. Such is not the case! The person just getting acquainted with golf is not yet really playing the game.

The glossary has been increased and now includes over one hundred definitions. Certain changes have been made in the rules section with additions and clarifications. For instance, revised and additional drawings with explanations are provided to clarify the oft-misunderstood rules on water and lateral water hazards.

We feel that this text performs a unique service in including a section on safety. In our experience we have seen students become teachers within twenty-four hours after having had their first golf lesson. This places us in a position of great responsibility. We are responsible for our students' safety and for the safety of each student's student. While it is true that relatively few accidents happen in golf, we urge you not to look upon the safety section lightly. Please do not start learning golf or teaching golf to a relative or friend until you have studied the safety precautions.

The problem of teaching or explaining a motor skill, such as the golf swing, is exemplified in the following story. An experienced and well-regarded professional was conducting a class for adults. On this particular day the nine-year-old niece of one student was visiting the class. The nine-year old and the students had practiced hitting golf balls, and then were called together for a talk by the professional. The teacher, also an excellent golfer, is exceptionally proficient in explaining the technique of swinging a golf club. After a fine talk to the class, the professional asked if the students understood the explanations. The adult members had no questions —they were ready and anxious to apply the information to hitting the golf ball. But the nine-year-old spoke up with her question: "Yes . . . but, how do you hit the darn thing?" This is a question we would all like answered. This book will not really tell you how to "hit the darn thing," but it will give you fundamentals, guides, and insights into learning and developing skill in hitting the golf ball. This book is intended to be a supplement to golf instruction. Because so many theories about the golf swing exist, no single book could be all-inclusive. The reader should not conclude that concepts and ideas left out of this text are necessarily questioned or rejected by the writers.

To accomplish the second purpose of the book, to help the reader become a more intelligent student of the game—better able to learn and develop skill in the strokes—revisions and additions have been made to the text. Drawings have been revised, and photographs and drawings have been added. The reader will find swing sequence photos of leading playing professionals interesting to study. Practice suggestions have been added so there are now about fifty interesting and sound ideas the reader can use to set up a program of practice—an absolute "must" for developing skill. A new section on self-coaching has been added. We think you will agree that following your class or private lessons, your future golf game will be most influenced by your own practice and your own self-coaching.

The section on error shots and their corrections has been extended. The errors of topping, "fat" shots, shanking, push, slice, pull, and hook are explained. Through drawings and explanations we invite the reader to join in this study. We try to look at the exact causes of the fault and then think about possible corrections of the errors. Through this book we, the authors, cannot see the student make the error so we readily admit our limitations. We present ideas for corrections, not absolute corrections. It has been our experience to see golfers thoroughly mystified by errors such as topping or slicing and as a result ready to abandon the game forever. We do not think this is necessary. We believe any player can do a lot to help himself with the use of common sense and understanding, but we do respect the importance of having a competent instructor observe the golf swing and make corrections.

We have retained our original concept of presenting the golf strokes. After a short discussion of certain fundamentals of learning and of swinging the golf club, we progress to learning the grip, stance, and the swings— working from the simple to the more complex. We have tried to draw upon your present knowledge, to relate skills you already possess to skills detailed here, and to keep in mind what is physically and mentally possible for a person to do. We have tried to emphasize that the golf swing is a whole movement, not a lot of pieces that you must put together. We want you to know that you cannot intellectualize all of learning—much will occur naturally with no thought given it. We know you must be patient in learning golf—yet you must be confident.

We feel that the information in this book will aid you in developing skill in the game, and we are certain that if you follow the information pertaining to knowledge of golf as a game, you can become a golfer with a 'touch of class.'

The game of golf

1

Golf is a game, a profession, a business asset, a social activity, and often a humiliating experience. The "put-down" that golf renders to all players may be its fascination. Golf teases you. It can lift you into ecstatic worlds where you dream of playing perfect golf. Then without warning your dreams are shattered—golf has put you in your place. Time and again the game seems to delight in proving that you can only be its devotee—not its master. After your visions of playing great golf are dimmed, you manage to stroke some shots with unusual skill. Again you are coaxed back into the imaginary world of perfect golf. Such is the lure of golf—sampling the joy of hitting fine shots, followed by great hopes, disappointments, and renewed hopes. The spirit and desire to attempt to conquer this challenging game survive despite all of its vicissitudes.

You are either one of the millions of people playing golf or you soon will be. It is not necessary to "sell" golf. The advantages of knowing how to play are evident. Ever-increasing numbers of people choose to learn golf and once chosen, golf becomes an enjoyable, lifetime recreation.

THE GAME

The object of golf is to play a round, usually 18 holes, in as few strokes as possible. At the beginning of each hole you are allowed to tee the ball so it is slightly elevated from the turf. After you strike the ball from the tee, you must then play the ball as you find it (except as otherwise provided in the rules), and continue doing so, in your turn, until you hit the ball into the hole (cup) which is sunk in a carpet-like area known as the putting green. The position of the cup is marked by a flagstick surmounted by a pennant. Usually the number of the hole is indicated on the pennant. The closely mowed area of grass between the tee and the putting green is called the fairway. The game would be relatively simple if you only had to play the ball from the tee, the fairway, and the putting green. But such is not the case. If you hit a shot off line and out of the fairway, you are likely to find your ball among trees and in long, thick grass—the rough. Because of a poorly hit or misjudged shot your ball may land in a creek, lake, or sand trap. You can be sure that, thanks to these and other possible occurrences, playing the game of golf will test your skill and your character.

After you complete play of each hole you record the number of strokes you have taken on a score card (see Etiquette—Putting Green). You add your scores for each nine holes and then total these figures for your 18-hole score.

Even though you usually play golf in a group of four, golf is a personal game. From the time you hit the ball off the first tee until you remove it from the cup on the eighteenth green you are in command of your game. You do not react to a moving ball someone else has hit or thrown. Nongolfers may scoff at the game: "What's so difficult about hitting a ball that is sitting still? . . . after all you know where the ball is and can position yourself to hit it." You can bet these same people will question the sense of such statements when they try to hit a ball that rests so very still. In golf if the ball is missed completely or is hit poorly, one cannot dismiss the incident by saying the opponent hit a superb shot. Allowed no excuses, the golfer must face the inert ball again. But when the golfer hits excellent shots, the game rewards him—he can claim credit for his fine play.

Not only is the golfer confronted with the problem of overcoming the inertia of the ball—he performs in a silent atmosphere wherein he is sensitive to everything both inside and outside of himself. Having time to think and act in quiet surroundings adds a singular dimension—one demanding concentration and self-discipline during the making of every shot. No shot is played without some thought. This is not so in many games where brilliant plays may be or must be executed as a result of reaction only. The golfer must plan the play, control his thinking, initiate and complete the action in order to play each golf shot. He has time to be introspective—which can be either a detriment or an advantage. He can "talk himself" into a bad shot, or a good shot.

All players admire and respect the skill of the tournament professionals, but in the last analysis the most important subject of thought and conversation for each golfer is: "My game."

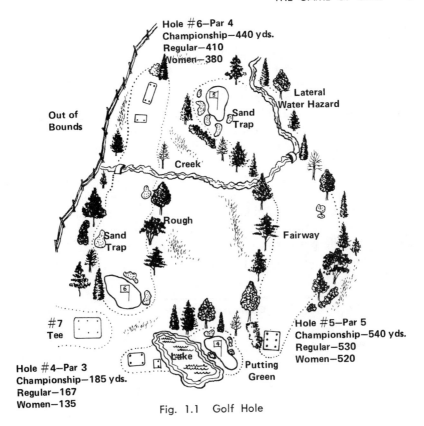

Hole #6—Par 4
Championship—440 yds.
Regular—410
Women—380

Lateral
Water Hazard

Out of
Bounds

Sand
Trap

Creek

Rough

Fairway

Sand
Trap

#7
Tee

Hole #5—Par 5
Championship—540 yds.
Regular—530
Women—520

Lake

Putting
Green

Hole #4—Par 3
Championship—185 yds.
Regular—167
Women—135

Fig. 1.1   Golf Hole

Play U.S.G.A. Rules except as modified by Local Rules.   Please Observe Rules of Etiquette.

		1	2	3	4	5	6	7	8	9	OUT	10	11	12	13	14	15	16	17	18	IN	TOTAL	HDCP.	NET
Yards - Championship - Blue		525	430	405	185	540	440	160	380	440	3505	505	420	180	535	455	210	400	435	442	3582	7087		
Regular	White	510	415	400	167	530	410	150	370	420	3372	490	385	165	520	423	185	375	415	428	3386	6758		
PAR		5	4	4	3	5	4	3	4	4	36	5	4	3	5	4	3	4	4	4	36	72		
Handicap*		11	5	15	7	9	1	13	17	3		10	16	14	8	2	12	18	6	4				
HOLE		1	2	3	4	5	6	7	8	9	OUT	10	11	12	13	14	15	16	17	18	IN	TOTAL	HDCP.	NET
Yards - Women	Red	480	375	395	135	520	380	147	365	380	3177	470	360	140	510	375	180	370	395	415	3215	6392		
PAR		5	4	4	3	5	4	3	4	4	36	5	4	3	5	4	3	4	4	5	37	73		
Handicap*		5	13	1	17	3	11	7	15	9		8	12	18	6	16	4	14	2	10				

Date _____   Scorer _____   Attest _____

Course Rating**
Men 69.8 - Women 70.6

Please Replace Divots....Repair Ball Marks on Greens....Rake Sand Traps
Slow Players Must Allow Following Group To Play Through

*Handicap—These numbers indicate the ranking of the golf holes in order of difficulty. Hole #6, HDCP. rating #1, is considered the most difficult hole for men. Hole #3 is rated the most difficult for women. Holes #16 and #12, HDCP. rating #18 for men and women respectively, are considered the least difficult.

**Course Rating—Evaluation of the playing difficulty of a course compared with other rated courses.

Fig. 1.2   Sample Score Card

THE GOLF COURSE

Much expert knowledge and work go into building and maintaining a golf course. Sometimes the playing of the game is so absorbing or exasperating that the beauty and design of a golf course are forgotten momentarily. Golf requires the largest playing field of any modern game. All courses and all holes differ. The architect designs the course to challenge you to hit your best shots and to penalize you if you fail to do so. He lays out the course taking full advantage of the topography, the beauty of nature and of the outdoors.

Whenever you play golf you have a universal opponent—par. Par scores are good scores. The major guide in determining par for a hole is the distance of the hole. The number of strokes a good player needs to hit the ball onto the putting green is figured, and then two strokes are added for play on the putting green. On the average, men hit the ball farther than women do, so women's par will be different than men's par on some of the holes.

COMPUTATION OF PAR

	Women		Men
Par		Par	
3	up to 210 yards	3	up to 250 yards
4	211-400	4	251-470
5	401-575	5	471 and over
6	576 and over		

Courses having all short holes, near 100 yards, offer certain advantages to the novice. A simpler version of golf is played, thus more success and pleasure are possible for the beginner. For all players these short courses are challenging, offer practice in the important short game, and require less time for the completion of a round.

On what may be called standard courses, holes vary in length from about 100 yards to about 600 yards. Since golf does not have an exact regulation playing field, the golfer must continually adapt his game to the peculiarities of each course, which may in itself vary in length and challenge from day to day. To protect the turf on the teeing area and around the cup on the putting green, the tee markers and the cups are shifted often. If the teeing areas and the putting greens are large, placement of both tee markers and cups can make a significant difference in the lengths of the holes.

Some golf courses have extra long teeing areas or have more than one tee per hole. On these courses three sets of tee markers may be set up:

blue markers for the back tees—the championship course; white markers for the middle tees—the regular course; and, red markers for the front tees—the women's course. (The colors of the markers may vary from course to course.) Many courses have only two sets of tees, regular and women's tees.

The changing of the cups on the putting greens from flat to various undulating surfaces adds challenge and zest to the game. On many courses, especially those bordering the ocean or in the mountains, the ball may roll over the slanting surfaces in a direction exactly opposite to the one figured on by the player after careful judgment of the slope. There is a story that after one man played an ocean-side course for the first time, he became so frustrated trying to figure out the roll of the ball on the greens that he returned the next day with a carpenter's level to check the slopes of the putting greens. (The rules of golf do not permit the use of such a device.)

Golf is not all of life, but to have the opportunity to play outstandingly beautiful and ability-testing courses throughout the world is enriching life for an increasing number of people.

THE GOLF CLUBS

You are permitted to carry a maximum of fourteen clubs when you play golf. All players do not use a full set, and players using a full set do not all select the same clubs. However, the usual set of fourteen clubs consists of one putter, nine irons, and four woods.

The Putter

This club is carried by every golfer, and it is the one club used most often. You use the putter to roll the ball relatively short distances into the hole. It is used principally on the putting green and from near it. The putter has a short shaft and an almost vertical face. Aside from these two points there is great variation in the design and construction of putters: the shaft may be attached to any part of the clubhead; the size and contour of the grip may be different than the standard grip of the woods and irons; the clubhead may be constructed in a variety of shapes.

Fig. 1.3   Types of Putters

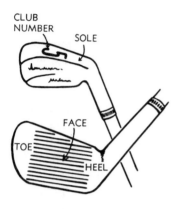

Fig. 1.4   Parts of Clubhead

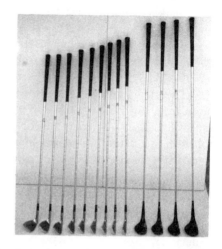

Fig. 1.5   Complete Set of Woods and Irons.

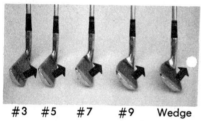

#3   #5   #7   #9   Wedge

Fig. 1.6   Club Face Loft—Irons

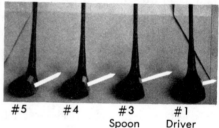

#5   #4   #3   #1
                        Spoon   Driver

Fig. 1.7   Club Face Loft—Woods

The Irons

The popular matched set of irons consists of eight clubs, numbered 2 through 9. The number 2 iron has the longest shaft and the least loft to the club face. As the club number goes up—3, 4, 5, etc.,—the shaft decreases in length, the angle of club-face loft increases, and the distance obtainable decreases. Therefore there is a great variation in the distance and the trajectory of the golf shots that can be hit with the different irons. There is a distance differential of approximately 10 yards between each of the irons. If you can hit a 5-iron shot 130 yards, you then can figure that you should hit a 4-iron 140 yards, and a 6-iron 120 yards. A special iron, a wedge, with a heavier flange and greater loft than the 9-iron is included in some matched sets. This club may be a pitching, sand, or dual-purpose wedge. If the wedge is not included in the matched set, the experienced golfer usually adds this club to complete his set of fourteen clubs.

A 2-iron is not especially favored by some people, so there are matched sets of irons available numbered 3 through 9. Besides the wedges, various special irons are made for short distance shots. Irons with medium loft and relatively short shafts are used to play low trajectory shots (run-up) to the green. These clubs are marketed under various names but are generally called "chippers." (In the past, irons were referred to by name, e.g., #2—mid-iron, #5—mashie, #9—niblick. Today you will seldom hear any numbered iron called by name.)

The Woods

Matched sets of woods are usually made up of four clubs, numbers 1, 3, 4, and 5. Formerly, the 2-wood was included in all sets, but because of its limited usefulness it has declined in popularity. The shafts of the woods are longer than those of the irons so you can expect to hit the ball farther with these clubs than with the irons. Like the irons, the different numbered woods vary in shaft length and club-face loft. The almost vertical face of the driver restricts its use to hitting the ball from a tee. There is a distance differential of approximately 10 yards between each of the different numbered woods.

Special woods numbering beyond the number 5 wood are available. Golfers who find it difficult to hit long irons prefer to use the more lofted woods for these distance shots. The numbers 1, 2, and 3 woods are referred to by both number and name—driver (1), brassie (2), and spoon (3). However, the trend is to refer to all clubs, except the putter and wedge, by number.

Beginner's Set

An excellent set of clubs for the novice consists of seven clubs: putter, numbers 3, 5, 7, and 9 irons, and numbers 1 and 3 woods. A five-club set, eliminating the 1-wood and 9-iron, also makes a suitable set for the beginner. (For information on club selection, see chapter 10.)

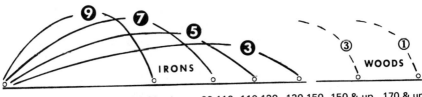

Average Golfer						
— Women	70-80 yds.	90-110	110-130	130-150	150 & up	170 & up
— Men	90-110 yds.	110-120	130-150	150-165	180 & up	200 & up

Fig. 1.8   Approximate Distances—Irons and Woods

Safety—your
most important lesson

2

Considering the number of people participating in golf, relatively few accidents occur. When accidents do occur, however, they can be serious. Most result from carelessness and lack of knowledge. You have a responsibility for your safety and the safety of others. Learn the following rules and *take no chances where safety is concerned.*

1. If you are a member of an instructional class, follow the precautions given you.
2. Before you swing any club, check to see that no one is within range of your swing.
3. When someone swings a club, be careful where you stand or walk. Stay well out of range of any swing.
4. Do not swing a club so that the follow-through is directed toward someone. A divot or an unseen pebble or rock might be hit toward someone. Also, though it is not likely to happen, the club could break or it could slip out of your hands.
5. Do not stand or walk ahead of a player taking a stroke that may endanger you. Similarly, when you are about to hit a ball that could endanger someone, make sure that no one is standing or walking ahead of you.
6. Before playing any stroke on the course, make certain the group ahead is out of range of your intended shot. Before attempting to play a shot to the putting green, wait until the group ahead has left the

green and is safely out of range. An errant shot in the direction of players walking off the green can endanger them. When your group completes play on the green, replace the flagstick, and leave the green immediately. (See Etiquette—Putting Green)

7. If you hit a ball that travels toward someone and may endanger that person, call "FORE!" loudly so that he will be alerted.

8. At the practice range, stay on the tee line. Do not walk ahead of the line to retrieve balls or tees.

9. When someone is teaching you or you are teaching someone, stand opposite the person, facing him. Do not stand on his right or left side in the path of the swing.

10. Lightning storms are dangerous on the golf course. The best precaution to follow is to avoid playing when such storms occur. Detailed precautions for protection from lightning when out on the course are given in the U.S.G.A. rule book.

11. If you use a motorized cart to drive around the course, drive with care.

Many people carry personal liability insurance for protection in case accidents do happen. The protection offered by these policies may merit your investigation and consideration.

When played knowledgeably, with alertness and common sense, golf is a safe game.

On learning golf

3

THE ABILITY TO IMITATE

You cannot help but use your ability to imitate in learning golf. You will "absorb" to varying degrees the golf swings you see. Imitation can be either an aid or a hindrance to learning. Young people, especially, imitate easily and to a high degree. Unlike some adults, they do not imitate on the intellectual or analytical level, but rather on a "subconscious" level. There is a quick grasp of the *movement as a whole*. Pictures and feelings are registered, but not in words. Many caddies and young people have imitated fine golf swings, and this imitation has played a part in their developing into good golfers.

Whether or not you possess a great deal of imitative ability, you can learn to make the best use of that which you have. Just as important, you can avoid complicating your learning by poor imitation. When you watch a golf swing, do not look for or try to copy small points of style, minor details of motion, or mannerisms and idiosyncracies. Keep in mind that *the golf swing is one motion*. If you see and have a "feel"* for the whole of a good swing—its design, pattern, rhythm, timing, power, and ease—then imitation can be an aid to learning.

SWINGING A GOLF CLUB

The "How" of Swinging

The beginning adult student of golf wants to know "how" to swing a golf club. This too often means that he wants to know all of the intricate

*Kinesthetic sense.

details of the swing—the complex analysis of the whole movement. Even if such an analysis were possible, then what? It takes about two seconds to make the golf swing. How much can one think about and then translate into action in that amount of time? Skillful movement is beautiful and complex—a real accomplishment. Lucky for us that we do not have to send conscious messages to all body parts, and at the correct split second, to make a golf swing. If this were necessary, no one could execute a satisfactory swing. Yet, this is what some beginners think they must do.

Questions of whether the swing is natural or unnatural are meaningless. The golf swing has been learned and executed well by people of all ages—even by those with physical handicaps. Some people experience difficulty in learning the golf swing, but this is not due to the movement. Trying to execute the "how" of the swing by performing numerous details of action is one of the chief reasons for problems in learning. Trying to think of and perform many parts of the swing in two seconds is not only impossible but also frustrating and tension-producing. Discomfort, irritation, and exhaustion are some of the results, but learning golf is not among them.

Overemphasizing one physical detail of the swing also causes trouble. For example, no one will question that the left arm remains fairly straight during a golf swing (putting excepted). The cue "left arm straight" is one of the most famous "hows" of executing golf swings. When this cue is carried beyond the correct position of easy extension to a stiff, tense position, learning the whole swing is not only difficult but almost impossible. Remember: your objective is to develop a golf swing—a whole unit of motion—not just a detail, and not a succession of details.

A good golfer performs details of action to which he has never given any thought. These actions are the result of swinging the club to stroke the ball to a predetermined target. The purpose of the movement is an important factor in determining the pattern and form of the motion produced. Suppose you wish to throw a ball straight up into the air. With this as the purpose, the arm swings up sharply and the body weight shifts upward with the arm motion. This coordination happens naturally. You neither think of swinging your arm up nor do you think of shifting your weight upward. You think about throwing the ball straight up into the air. If you thought of and carefully concentrated on the details of what the body and its parts do, would you be more effective in throwing the ball skyward? Keeping the objective of golf in mind—stroking the ball to a target—will help you develop the golf swing. Many of the details that you may now think are necessary "hows" of the swing will occur. They will take their places as part of the whole swing, as you concentrate on swinging to stroke the ball to a target. In learning the golf swings, do not only try to intellectualize the process. Place some trust in your body's ability to take care of details. Permit learning to take place.

Mechanics of the Swing

Incorrect information or lack of information concerning certain mechanics of the swing misleads not only the beginner but also the experienced player. This discussion presents certain fundamentals of the movement of the club and its contact with the ball. The purpose of discussing these mechanics is to prevent incorrect concepts and thus incorrect efforts. The correct basic concepts of clubhead motion and ball contact serve as a base for learning and developing an effective golf swing.

Clubhead Speed   It is a great pleasure to hit a golf ball a long distance—the desire of all golfers. But this desire has ruined many golf swings because of faulty attempts at getting distance. The important factor in determining the distance the golf ball will travel is the speed of the clubhead at ball contact. This speed is directly related to the size of the arc of the swing. When you wish to stroke a ball a short distance, you choose a short club, grip down on the handle, and take a short swing. When you wish to stroke a ball a long distance, you choose a long club, hold it at its full length, and take a full swing. The clubhead will travel at a higher rate of speed in the full swing, and thus the golf ball will travel a greater distance. With the longer clubs you should hit the ball longer distances, but this does not always happen. Why? If you are not getting greater distance with a longer club, then you must be doing something to *prevent* the clubhead from developing its maximum speed at contact with the ball. Usually the fault lies in incorrect muscular *exertion*. Preparing to "hit hard" and exerting yourself with sudden and violent efforts at ball contact result in less clubhead speed and loss of control of the club. The timing and smooth blending of forces that come with correct muscular effort, together with the size of the arc of the swing, produce clubhead speed and distance. Do not be misled into thinking that it is recommended that you swing slowly when you take the full swing. The opposite is recommended. Let the clubhead speed develop—do not prevent it through unnecessary exertion.

The Pattern of the Swing   If you consider two movements with which you are familiar, then the arc of the swing may be better understood. Assume you are going to throw a baseball underhand. What path does your hand take? It swings up as you swing your arm back in preparation for the throw. Then after the release of the ball your hand swings up on the follow-through. You do not think about and try to swing your hand *up*. That is a *result* of your purpose—not the purpose itself. Now assume you are going to bat a baseball. In preparation for the hit, you swing the bat in an arc back around you. On the follow-through after striking the ball, the bat again swings in an arc around you. You do not make any special effort to swing the bat in this pattern.

In the golf swing you have a combination of these two arcs because the ball is on or near the ground. The swing of the clubhead upward and around you is again the *result* of your purpose. The circular pattern is a natural result of your standing in a fairly fixed position to strike the ball from the ground to a target. The arc is not something you set out to copy exactly (fig. 3.1).

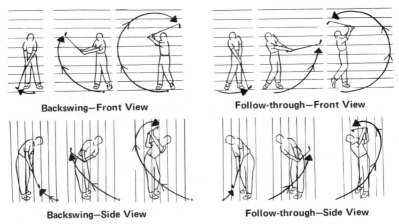

Backswing—Front View   Follow-through—Front View

Backswing—Side View   Follow-through—Side View

Fig. 3.1   Swing Arc.

Through the contact area the clubhead travels close to the ground. Because the clubhead travels in an arc around you, it enters the contact area from inside the intended line of flight, travels on the intended line of flight, and then on the follow-through again travels inside the intended line of flight. This is the natural outcome of a good swing (fig. 3.2).

Fig. 3.2   Path of Clubhead Through Contact Area.

Ball Contact   The direction and flight of the ball can be directly related only to the contact of the club face with the ball. Other factors may affect this contact, but they in themselves do not propel the ball—only the club face can do that. If at ball contact the face of the club is traveling

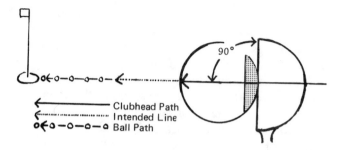

Clubhead Path
Intended Line
Ball Path

Fig. 3.3   Impact Producing Straight Shot to Target.

on the intended line of flight and the face is at right angles to the line, then the ball will travel straight along the intended line toward the target. The two factors determining the direction the ball will travel are (1) the path of the clubhead, and (2) the position of the club face in relation to the path of the clubhead (fig. 3.3).

When you studied the illustrations showing the club-face loft of each of the iron and wood clubs, you learned that when the ball is hit properly, the slant of the club face will determine the trajectory of the ball. You do not attempt to hit the ball into the air—the club face is designed to do this for you when the ball is hit. It is common to hear a struggling player complain: "I can't get the ball up," or "I can't get under the ball." Until this person stops trying to propel the ball upward and starts permitting the club face to loft the ball, his troubles will continue and probably increase. This understanding is basic to your hitting good golf shots: *the club face—not a special effort on your part—lofts the ball into flight.*

A small error in contact with the ball may cause a great error in shot result. Golf requires a high degree of accuracy. You will get various shot results in your early attempts to strike the ball. This should not discourage or frustrate you. Considering the size of the golf ball and the small hitting area of the club face, the wonder is that so many fine golf shots are made.

Progession in Learning the Swings

If you have watched champion golfers prepare to play a round of golf, you have observed that they start their practice using the medium or short irons. They hit shots requiring less than the full swing and then work to the longer swings and the longer clubs. This makes sense. The short swing is an important stroke of the game. The "feel" and touch for all golf swings is best found and recovered in these short strokes. Short swings serve as easy muscle and joint "warm-up" for the full swing.

The foregoing statements may be used to support this opinion: *if it is best to start learning golf with a particular swing, then the choice should be the small swing.* It is not suggested that the beginner delay working on the longer swing and the full swing but a little patience is recommended

—walk before you run. You are apt to have more success in striking the ball with the less complex short swing than with the full swing. Success in striking the ball makes learning more enjoyable as well as more effective. The putting stroke can be learned and practiced right along with the other strokes.

THE REAL SECRET

Useful guides can be given for learning golf and executing the swings, but no exact formula can be proposed. Who can confidently say he has all the answers to learning golf or to consistently hitting fine golf shots? The novice watches the champion, notes a detail of the swing, and hopefully thinks he has "discovered the secret" of good golf. Of one thing you can be sure—the champion does not want to know *this secret!* The champion already knows the REAL SECRET—following the fundamentals of good form in the grip, stance, and swing—and hitting thousands of golf balls in practice and play.

Pictures by Irv Schloss. Courtesy of Faultless Golf Products, Division of Abbott Laboratories.

LEE TREVINO

Addressing the ball

4

Taking the correct grip and the proper stance are the essential preliminary steps in executing successful golf shots with the irons and the woods. Some golf shots may be hit well when it appears that the fundamentals of grip and stance are defied, but defiance of the fundamentals only serves to tear apart a golf swing, because compensations must be made *constantly* to counteract errors. Your objective is to develop a sound swing and game that will improve with practice. Give yourself the best chance to do this. Start with the correct grip and stance.

THE GRIP

Types of Grip

The *overlapping grip* is the most widely used. In this grip, the little finger of the right hand rests on or overlaps the index finger of the left hand. In the *interlocking grip* the little finger of the right hand and the index finger of the left hand interlock. One advantage of either of these two positions is that there is a feeling of unity between the hands because of the overlapping or interlocking of the fingers. An advantage claimed for the overlapping grip is that you have both index fingers on the shaft. The index fingers along with the thumbs are key fingers in holding anything. A person with small hands and short fingers may prefer the interlocking grip. Various names have been given the grip in which all the fingers of both hands are placed on the club. One claim made for this grip is that it is a strong one. The person who lacks some grip strength or who has small hands may find the 10-finger grip most suitable.

Individual preference, "feel," strength, and the size of hands may all be factors in choosing the best grip for you. It is important to note that the three positions are very much alike; the only difference between them is the placement of the little finger of the right hand and the index finger of the left hand. All three grips have been used successfully; however, the overlapping grip is favored by the majority of golfers.

Overlapping   Interlocking   "10-Finger"

Fig. 4.1   Types of Grips

Taking the Correct Grip

1. Place the sole of the club flat on the ground and support the tip of the handle with your right hand.

2. Let your left hand hang at your side. Note the natural hanging position of the left hand and arm.

Fig. 4.2

3. Without changing the natural hanging position of the left hand, move it forward to the club so that the club handle extends across the middle section of the index finger and back across the palm (fig. 4.2). The hand, arm, and shoulder should still be in an easy, relaxed position.

4. The back of the left hand faces the intended line of ball flight. Be certain of this. Do not have the back of the left hand facing the ground with the palm pointing skyward.

5. Keeping the left hand in the proper position and relaxed, close the fingers and take hold of the club handle (fig. 4.3). Hold the

Fig. 4.3

club with some firmness, but not with great tension. Holding the club with the left hand, you should be able to move the clubhead easily. Try moving the clubhead just a few inches back and forth on the ground while maintaining this correct grip.

Fig. 4.4

6. Now, let the right arm hang easily at your side. Note its natural hanging position.

7. Without changing the natural hanging position of the right hand, move the hand to the club so that the club handle lies across the middle part of the index finger. The life line of the right palm is superimposed over the left thumb (fig. 4.4).

8. The palm of the right hand faces the direction of the intended target. The palms of the hands face each other. Be certain of this. The right hand, arm, and shoulder should still be in an easy position.

Fig. 4.5

9. Close the fingers and palm of the right hand and take hold of the club (fig. 4.5). If you are taking the overlapping grip, allow the little finger of the right hand to fall naturally over the index finger of the left hand. If you are taking the interlocking grip, raise the index finger of the left hand and interlock it with the little finger of the right hand. It is important that you do not change the positions of the hands when you overlap or interlock the fingers.

10. Check the face of the club to see that it is square to the intended line of ball flight. Check the firmness of the grip and ease of motion by moving the clubhead a few inches back and forth along the ground.

Check Points—Left Hand   Take hold of the club, look down at your grip, and check the following points (fig. 4.6).

1. The **V** formed by the thumb and index finger points in the general area between the chin and the right shoulder. Checking where the **V** points is a matter of judgment. Follow your instructor's specific instructions.
2. The base segment of the thumb will touch the side of the hand, forming a line.
3. The left thumb is slightly to the right of the center of the shaft.
4. The knuckles at the base of the first two fingers can be seen, and perhaps the knuckle at the base of the third finger.
5. The tip of the thumb and tip of the index finger will lie close to each other.

Fig. 4.6
Left-hand Grip

Check Points—Right Hand (fig. 4.7)

1. The **V** formed by the thumb and index finger points in the general area between the chin and right shoulder. See left hand grip.
2. The base segment of the thumb will touch the side of the hand, forming a line.
3. The thumb is placed slightly to the left of center of the shaft.
4. The knuckle at the base of the index finger can be seen, and perhaps also the knuckle at the base of the long finger.

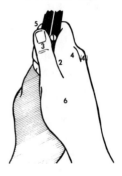

Fig. 4.7
Complete Grip

5. The tip of the thumb and the tip of the index finger lie close to each other. The tip of the thumb does not extend down the shaft beyond the middle segment of the index finger.
6. The left thumb fits in the life line of the right palm.

The left hand is a combination finger and palm grip. The right hand is mainly a finger grip.

The hands should feel like a single unit since they must work together.

Taking the correct grip is a basic and new skill to learn. Approach the learning in a relaxed manner. You may feel and say, "The grip is uncomfortable." You would be more correct to say that the grip is new and different. For some people, a grip that seems "comfortable" at this early stage in learning may not be a correct one. It does not follow, however, that the grip should feel awkward and difficult—it is new and will not feel as easy as holding a pencil.

The grip is for control, touch, and speed. Do not be misled by a feeling of not having a "good hold" on the club. A vise-like, tight grip makes swinging the club impossible. Holding the club with authority is necessary, but this authority is for swinging the club, not for crushing the shaft! Hold the club with the fingers and hands. Do not tense up other parts of the body as you grip the club.

The grip should remain the same throughout the swing. Avoid any tendency to release the hold on the club with the last three fingers of the left hand.

Try to avoid developing blisters on your hands. Wearing a glove either on the left hand or on both hands will provide some protection.

Relation of Hand Position to Directional Flight of Ball

The position of the hands on the club affects the directional flight of the ball. For instance, if the right hand is placed on the club so that the palm points skyward, the ball is likely to travel to the left of the target. The reason for this can be easily demonstrated. Grip the club with the right hand with the palm facing skyward and the club face square to the intended target. Keeping a firm grip, move the right hand over so the palm faces the intended line of ball flight. Note that the club face turns over and is in a closed position pointing to the left and downward. If either or both hands are placed on the club contrary to the natural hanging position, there will be a tendency for the hand or hands to return to the natural position during the swing, thereby changing the face of the club.

Hand position will not always determine the directional flight of the ball because various compensations and efforts may be made during the swing to affect the club face.

When your game has developed to the point where you have a fairly consistent stroke, you may at times wish to curve the ball to the right or left. A change in the grip could accomplish this for you. Changing the grip from the correct to the incorrect for eliminating errors in ball flight, however, is not recommended.

THE STANCE

Types of Stance

The usual way of classifying various stances is to draw a relationship between the line on which the feet are placed and the intended line of flight. In the square stance the feet are placed on a line parallel with the intended line of flight. This stance is the most widely used one. It is the most natural position to assume to strike the ball. Any great deviation from this square stance is a point of style or an idiosyncracy, and copying such a stance has no merit. If the stance is changed from the square position to an open or closed stance for certain shots, then the change should be slight. A square stance can be recommended for almost all golf shots.

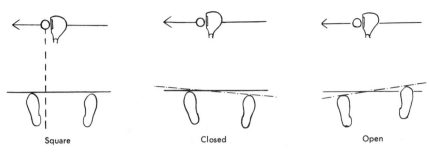

| Square | Closed | Open |

Fig. 4.8   Types of Stance

Stances vary in width for a logical reason—the width of the stance should fit the purpose of the swing. If you wish to hit a ball the maximum distance, your feet are placed approximately as far apart as your shoulders are wide. This stance will allow you to swing the club in a wide arc and to keep your balance while swinging the clubhead swiftly. If you wish to hit the ball a short distance you will swing the club in a small, controlled arc, and a narrow stance fits this purpose best. The same principle applies to the distance you stand from the ball. For distance shots, using the longer-shafted clubs, you will necessarily stand farther from the ball than you will for the shorter distance shots.

Taking the Stance

1. Aiming (Step 1, figs. 4.9 and 4.10)

    Visualize the shot you desire. Sight to the target. Draw an imaginary line through the ball to the target.

    Holding the club correctly, place the club sole flat on the ground back of the ball. The club face points to the intended target. The edge of the clubhead where the sole and face meet should be perpendicular to the intended line of flight.

2. Placing the Feet (Step 2, figs. 4.9 and 4.10)

    For a short approach shot, move your feet to a comfortable narrow stance. An open stance may be preferred for this shot.

| Step 1 | Step 2 | Step 1 | Step 2 |

Fig. 4.9   Taking Stance for
Short Approach Shot.

Fig. 4.10   Taking Stance for
Wood Shot.

21

For a wood shot, move your feet out to each side to a comfortable stance of approximately shoulder width.

If the clubhead is placed approximately opposite the center of the stance, the ball will be on a line from a point approximately opposite the inside of the left heel extending toward a point opposite the center of the stance. This is an ideal position for striking most golf shots. (See fig. 4.11.

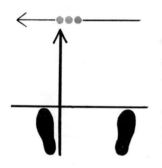

Wood Shot

Short Approach Shot

Fig. 4.11 Area of Ball Position.

Fig. 4.12 Addressing the Ball—Side View.

The action of first placing the clubhead back of the ball with the arms easily extended gives you a gauge for the distance you should stand away from the ball. If the feet are positioned first you may have to do considerable shifting back and forth to get to the correct distance from the ball.

For ease and comfort the toes should be turned out slightly and the weight should be about evenly distributed between the feet. The knees are slightly bent. This "give" of the knees is for comfort and readiness to swing the club.

The body is bent forward from the hip joints and the back is fairly straight, but not rigid. Avoid slumping and rounding the shoulders.

The arms should be free of the body and "feel" as though they are hanging from the shoulders. In this "hanging" position the arms will be naturally straight. Trying to hold the arms straight or "stiff" can be a hindrance to learning or performing the golf swing.

The Waggle and Forward Press

A waggle is a movement of the clubhead in preparation for swinging the club. It may be considered a rehearsal for the start of the backswing. After the stance is taken the clubhead is moved away a short distance from the ball in the path in which you intend to swing the club. Then it is moved forward to the ball or up over the ball and back to the address position. This gives you a "feel" of the club and a feeling of ease and confidence for starting the swing. The action of picking the club up and setting it down is not a waggle. Such nervous actions should be avoided. The waggle is not a necessary motion but rather an auxiliary one. As you progress in golf, you will develop a personal style for waggling the club.

A forward press is a movement of the body in preparation for starting the swing. It may be a subtle motion. Just before the swing is started there is a *slight* "give" of the right knee toward the left, thus the name of the action—a press forward. There is no exactness to this movement. Some fine players do not use a forward press. For some beginners a forward press may be a natural movement to make; for others it may be an awkward motion to attempt. If the forward press is not an easy, natural motion, it can best be postponed until such time as the player has had adequate experience in swinging the club.

PRACTICE SUGGESTIONS

1. Place your hands on the club, check the grip, and release the hold on the club. Practice taking the grip. Do not try to maintain what you think is the correct grip because you fear you will not get this correct grip again. A grip maintained for a period of time will become incorrect because of unconscious shifting of the hands and increased tension. The check points of the grip are simple to apply. If these are used you can be confident you will take a correct hold on the club.

2. In your early practice of taking the grip, follow the steps in the text: (1) place the left hand on the grip and check the hand position, (2) then place the right hand on the club and check the complete grip. The grip will become comfortable and easy with practice. After practice in taking the grip in two steps, take the grip almost simultaneously with both hands. Have a feeling of the two hands working together and fitting together on the club. There is no need to tense the fingers and hands until after you have checked the grip. After you check the hand positions and find them correct, then without changing the position, take a firm hold on the club.

3. Holding the club correctly, practice moving the clubhead in the air in various patterns. Write your name with the clubhead, draw circles with the clubhead, etc. Learn to feel control of the clubhead (fig. 4.13). These exercises are a good test of the grip in action. The wrists and arms must be relaxed and flexible while the correct hold on the club is maintained. Note that as you direct your attention to moving the clubhead, the wrists and arms move—a responsive action resulting from moving the clubhead.

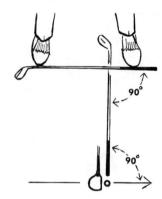

Fig. 4.13

Fig. 4.14 Checking Alignment with Golf Clubs.

4. Do exercises to develop grip and arm strength. Squeeze a sponge ball or a towel. Flex and extend the fingers and arms offering your own resistance to the movements. Plan a sensible exercise program that will increase your fitness for golf.

5. Address the ball and check the address position. As you do so "let go" especially through the shoulders so you will be relaxed and ready to move. Maintain a correct and firm grip.

6. Practice taking the stance to different targets. You can check to see if the stance is square by laying a club on the ground with the shaft touching the front tips of your shoes. Then step back of the ball and see if the club shaft is parallel with the intended line of flight (fig. 4.14).

7. Without holding a club, assume an easy, comfortable stance. Check: feet shoulder width apart, body bent forward from the hip joints, knees "easy," and arms hanging free of body. Swing arms a short distance back and forth. Watch a spot on the ground to maintain a steady head position. Let the body and legs "give" with the swing (see chaps. 5 and 6). Increase the arm swing to a point where one shoulder easily moves under the chin on the forward swing. This exercise is excellent for "warm-up" and for learning and registering the "feeling" of the free swinging of the arms and the correct "body posture in motion."

8. Make the steps in addressing the ball simple and concise. After you have had some practice in taking the stance avoid making a "production" of it. Place some trust in yourself to aim and to settle in a stance which is good for you.

Short approach shots

5

The short approach shots played to the putting green are pitch shots and chip (or run-up) shots. The pitch shot is played with a high lofted iron, thus the ball travels in a high trajectory and upon landing tends to stop with little or no forward roll. When a ball is contacted squarely with a lofted iron, the club face will compress the ball well below its center of gravity, thus imparting backspin to it. This backspin and the height from which the ball falls to the ground will tend to stop the forward motion of the ball when it lands. In some instances the ball will bounce backwards after landing.

The chip or run-up shot is usually stroked with a medium iron. The ball travels in a relatively low trajectory. The chip shot will, after landing, roll a longer distance than the pitch shot, due to the lack of backspin and to the low trajectory.

You do not need to learn two swings to hit the pitch and chip shots. The club-face loft—not the swing—produces the backspin and the trajectory of the ball. You have one swing to learn. Depending upon the desired distance, the swings will vary in length or circumference.

APPROACH SITUATIONS AND CLUB SELECTION

In certain approach situations there is little or no choice in the shot you must play. In situation A, figure 5.1, you must hit over a deep bunker, land the ball on the green, and have it stay there . . . use a high lofted iron and hit a pitch shot. In situation B, you must strike the ball so it will travel

low under the limbs of a tree . . . use an iron with little loft and play a
chip shot. In situation C, figure 5.2, the area of green to which you must
play the ball is small and the green slopes downhill . . . hit a run-up shot
into the bank of the hill so that the ball will bounce off the bank onto the
green.

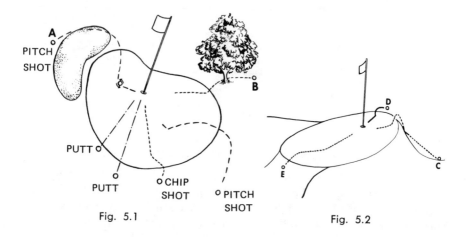

Fig. 5.1   Fig. 5.2

When there is a choice in the shot you can play, consider:

1.   *Your skill.* Use the club in which you have confidence and success.
     When practical to do so, choose the chip shot over the pitch shot.
     First, it is an easier shot for most golfers. Second, if an error such as
     topping or half-topping is made, the error in shot result is likely to
     be less with the chip shot. For a given distance a pitch shot must be
     struck with greater force than a chip shot. Thus, in the pitch shot if
     the ball is erroneously hit above center, it is likely to roll far past the
     hole and putting green.

2.   *The condition of the course.* If the putting green is dried out and hard,
     pitch shots will not "hold" on the green. Use run-up shots under these
     conditions. Ordinarily, do not use chip shots when the ground is very
     wet and soft.

3.   *The contour of the green and the position of the cup.* In the approach
     shot, allow for the ball to roll more when it lands on a downhill sur-
     face and to roll less when it lands on an uphill surface. In situation D,
     fig. 5.2, the surface is downhill and the hole is close to the edge of
     the green. Usually an iron with loft would be used to counteract the
     tendency of the ball to roll downhill. In situation E, a medium iron
     would be used for a run-up shot. The putting stroke may be your
     most effective approach when a lofted shot is not needed and when

the ball will roll easily on the grass (fig. 5.1 and 5.2). In situations D and E (fig. 5.2), most golfers will consider using either an approach iron or a putter. Their decision will be based on their experience in playing the stroke and on the situation, which includes the condition of the turf around the green.

4. *The lie of the ball.* If the ball is lying on thin turf or on bare ground, it usually is easier to stroke the ball effectively with a medium iron than with a high lofted iron.

THE SWINGS

The terms *one-quarter, one-half,* and *three-quarter* are often used to describe the approximate length of approach swings. You learn through practice and experience how far to swing the club for a given distance. You sight and judge the distance for a shot, and then through the remarkable sense of "feel," or kinesthetic sense, you swing the club the distance your eye, "feel," and experience indicate. There is a subconscious translation of this synthesis of judgments into the execution of the golf shot. At times all golfers experience the thrill of executing approach shots expertly—either by having the ball come to rest inches from the hole or by holing out the approach shot. (The three-quarter swing is discussed in chapter 6.)

Fig. 5.3   Approximate Quarter Swing

The Quarter Swing

Addressing the Ball

1. Take a square stance or a slightly open stance.
2. Grip down on the handle of the club.
3. Play the ball from an area extending from a point opposite the inside of the left heel to the center of the stance.

Backswing

1. Swing the clubhead back close to the ground.
2. Watch a spot on the back of the ball where you intend to strike it.
3. Concentrate on swinging the clubhead with a feeling of control in the hands.

Swing Through

1. Swing the clubhead close to the grass through the ball.
2. The ball will be in the way of the club face. Do not make a special effort to meet or hit the ball.
3. Try to watch the club face strike the ball.

Fig. 5.4   Half Swing

The Half Swing

Addressing the Ball (see Quarter Swing and chap. 4)

Backswing

1. This longer approach swing is a continuation of the smaller swing.
2. The intention and thought is to swing the clubhead away from the ball and distant target, and then toward the ball and the distant target. The clubhead will naturally swing inside the intended line of ball flight and up from the ground.

Swing Through

1. The club swings through close to the grass.
2. After the ball is struck, allow your head to turn naturally to see the shot result.

3. The whole swing feels smooth and continuous. The clubhead naturally gains momentum through the contact area.

Proper Swinging Results in Good Form

These swings should not be difficult to learn. They are simple, uncomplicated movements. The details of motion are the result of having the correct grip and stance and swinging the clubhead.

1. The clubhead is swung in a wide arc, keeping the same radius throughout the swing. Result—the left arm will maintain the easy extended position it assumed in addressing the ball.

2. During the swing there is a lack of tension in the shoulders and arms. Result—there is a free arm and shoulder motion in the swing.

3. The grip is correct and firm but not tense. Result—there will be a gradual bending of the wrists if the clubhead is swung. If the handle of the club is carried back and forth or if it is lifted, there can be no natural responsive action of the wrists. The cooperative action of the wrists becomes more apparent as the swing lengthens. Wrist action is a very gradual motion. It does not occur at a certain spot in the swing. There is no conscious effort to "use" the wrists.

4. The stance is comfortable and there is a slight bend to the knees. Result—there may be a slight give of the body towards the direction of the swing—but not a "give" of the head. As you swing back the left knee will naturally give to the right side. There will be a tendency for a slight weight shift to the right foot. As you swing through the opposite action occurs. Like the wrist motion, this action of the body and legs becomes greater and more evident as the swing lengthens.

No one detail of action takes place by itself. There is a *fusion* of all details into a unit of motion. A smooth swing is the result. The swing is efficient. *Only the movement necessary to accomplish the purpose of the swing is made.* There is less movement of the body and its parts in the small swings. As the swing increases in length the movement increases proportionately to produce and accommodate the motion. You can *allow* most of the correct movements—good form— to develop as a result of swinging the clubhead.

STROKE EXECUTION—SOME ANALYSIS AND DETAIL

Grip, Hand Action, and Wrist Action

If the grip is changed during the swing, an awkward action in the hands and wrists is almost certain to occur. You can check your swing at any point to see if your grip has remained correct. The check is exactly the same as the one used in the address position. Stop your swing at the point where you wish to check it, move your head so that you are looking at your grip, just as you did in the address position, and apply the check points to the grip. In this checking do not move your head until you stop the swing. Suppose you wish to check your grip at the end of the back-swing. Take the correct grip, address the ball properly, and swing the club back and stop. Hold this position. Turn your head to the side so it is in the same *relative position* to your hands as at the address. Now check the grip. The grip should be the same on the club handle as at the address.

A common fault in making the swing for short approach shots is that of attempting to scoop the ball up into the air. In this erroneous action, the hands work in opposition to each other in the contact area. The right hand moves forward and under, as the left hand holds back. Through the vital impact area hands *must* move with the club (see chap. 9, fig. 9.2). At times there may even be a feeling of the hands leading the club. If you find that you are striking the ground with the clubhead before you strike the ball, you can suspect that you are trying to scoop the ball. If you will *let* the clubhead do the work for which it was designed, and not try to loft the ball, you can avoid this error.

You can easily check and rehearse the wrist action that occurs in the swing. Keeping the arms extended as in the address position, raise the clubhead and point it forward and then over your right shoulder. As a result of moving the clubhead the wrists will bend. Note that if you lift the club handle with the arms there will be no bending of the wrists (fig. 5.5).

Fig. 5.5 Wrist Action Exercise

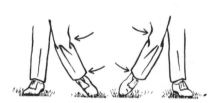

Fig. 5.6 Foot and Leg Action Exercise.

Sharon Miller, Member Advisory Staff, Ping Golf Clubs (Karsten Mfg. Corp.)

Knee Action and Foot Action

Action of the knees, feet, and legs is a part of swinging the clubhead in a certain direction. Because of previously developed muscle habits and tension there might be a lack of response in developing this combined action. Rather than complicating the swing by thinking of how to move your feet or which foot to move, this part of the swing can be practiced by itself without breaking up the blending action of all parts of the swing. A simple practice exercise is to alternate bending the left knee toward a spot in front of the right foot, and then bending the right knee so that it points to a spot in front of the left foot. Accompanying this knee bending is some inward action of the ankle and foot. The weight shifts to the inner border of the foot and big toe. The heel may raise slightly from the ground with the inner border raising less than the outer border. When you have trained your muscles to move in this manner and have developed a "feeling" for the motion, then you can expect to get the correct action of legs and feet when you swing the club. This practice exercise plus the directional influence of the swing will help develop a correct and natural action.

Head Position

In all golf swings the head remains in a fairly stationary position until after the ball is struck. After you contact the ball, your head will turn naturally to accomodate the follow-through of the swing. There should be no question about this correct mechanical aspect of the swing. The cue "watch the ball until you strike it" accomplishes the steady head position for most people. The cue "keep your head down" can result in serious errors if the idea is overemphasized. If one were to keep his head down so that his chin is resting on his chest, it would be impossible to make a good golf swing. As the body turns during the swing the shoulder moves under the chin. The "head down" position tends to block what would be the natural movement of the shoulders and body. One other serious error that may result from exaggerating this cue is moving the head down and lower during the backswing. This binds the backswing. Then, because the head must be moved back up into the address position when the ball is struck, the control and the momentum of the clubhead are destroyed. Until after impact your head should remain still and in the position it is in at the address. However, you should not hold yourself rigid; neither should you concentrate solely on the position of your head.

PRACTICE SUGGESTIONS

1. Practice swinging all you can. Swing the clubhead back and forth in a pendulum manner, cutting and sweeping the grass with each back

and forth movement. When you practice swinging continuously, the speed of the clubhead will be the same for both the backswing and the swing through. This does not happen in a single swing, because the clubhead accelerates through the impact zone. When you take one swing at a time, watch the clubhead sweep the grass then hold the finish of your swing momentarily, feeling control of the club with your hands.

2. Hit many chip shots from near the green. Practice until you are machinelike in performance so that there need be no thought regarding the execution of the shot. Aim to roll the ball into the cup, and if the ball does not drop into the cup, have it come to rest very close to the hole. You may find it helpful to pick out a spot on the green where you wish to have the ball land.

3. Work from short approaches to longer ones. Change your target both for distance and line of direction. Learn to aim and judge distance. Make mental notes on the different length shots, i.e., how much to "choke up" on the grip; the width of the stance; the necessary length of swing.

4. Practice stroking the ball from good lies on the turf. When you increase your skill, try stroking the ball from good and poor lies. Stroking the ball from other than a good lie is not so much a matter of learning how to do it but rather a matter of facing the situation without anxiety. Practice from various lies, but do not continue practice from poor lies if you are not having success. Such practice tends to destroy confidence and disrupt a good swing pattern.

5. Practice both chip shots and pitch shots. In changing from hitting chip shots to hitting pitch shots, you may "feel" a difference in the swings. For example: you are chipping shots 30 yards with a 5-iron, you then change to a 9-iron or wedge to pitch the same distance. When you use the higher lofted iron for the pitch shot, it will be necessary to take a longer swing. You have already noted that there is more responsive wrist action as the swing lengthens, so naturally you might sense more wrist action in the pitch shot. The longer swing and the differences in clubhead weights and shaft lengths all contribute to what you sense about the stroke. This is a result—to purposely try to develop two different swings for the chip shot and the pitch shot is neither necessary nor recommended. Postpone practice with the wedge until you have developed some real skill with the other short irons.

6. In your practice take a comfortable stance. You may prefer a slightly open stance, but do not adopt one which is not "easy" for you. You must be in balance and comfortable to hit these delicate shots. It is

From a target, pace off or measure distances of 20, 30, and 40 yards. Practice both chip shots and pitch shots from these distances.
1. Note the lengths of the swings you must take for the different shots.
2. Test your accuracy in hitting the shots. Hit a total of 30 balls, 10 from each distance. How many balls come to rest within 7 paces (approximately 20 feet) of the hole or target?
3. Check your progress. Keep a mental or written record of your practice.

possible to change the ball flight by changing the position from which you play the ball. If you play the ball from a point more nearly opposite to the right side of the stance, the ball will tend to travel in a low trajectory; a ball struck from a point more nearly opposite to the left side of the stance will tend to travel in a high trajectory. You have already learned that opening and closing the club face will also change the ball flight. After you have developed skill in swinging and in stroking the ball, this information on changing ball flight trajectory can be useful to you.

7. The following swinging exercises will help you develop a feeling of swinging the clubhead and sensing control in the fingers and hands.

   a. Reverse the club and grip the shaft near the clubhead so the end of the handle is about 6 inches from the ground. Swing the tip of the handle in the air back and forth continuously. Then reverse the club and take your regular grip on the handle and swing the clubhead. After continuous swinging practice, follow the same procedure of reversing the club, but take one swing at a time. You will definitely feel the clubhead after swinging the comparatively weightless handle.

   b. Practice the swinging as in (1) above, but with your eyes closed. You will note even greater sensitivity of clubhead control in the fingers and hands and of feeling the whole swing.

8. Short strokes are an important part of your game. Do not neglect them. Spend the first part of every practice session on these shots.

The full strokes— irons and woods

6

There is no difference in the way you swing the wood club and the full iron. The swings may feel different to you. This is reasonable, for there is a difference in shaft lengths, club balances, club weights, the speed of the swings, and the arc of the swings. In the wood swing the path of the club-head is closer and more level to the ground for a longer distance through the contact area than it is with the irons. The wood swing may feel more like a sweep than the swing with the irons. One often hears that in playing an iron there should be a feeling of hitting down on the ball. If exaggerated, this cue can lead to great trouble. The swing through the contact area, for both woods and irons, should be one of hitting the ball toward a distant target. The experienced golfer can try hitting down and because of his experience in handling a club, he may not encounter difficulty. For the novice who is trying to learn the swing, this idea of "hitting down" may result in a poor swing and a poor shot. The best idea for most players is to *hit the ball out toward the target*. The swing may feel downward, but do not try to force such an action.

THE IRONS

Distances and Club Selection

You will learn through practice how far you can hit with each iron. Until you gain some experience there probably will be little difference in the distance you can stroke the ball with the various clubs. You may get greater

Fig. 6.1   The Three-Quarter Swing.

distance with the medium irons than you do with the long irons. This should not concern you. After hitting many practice shots, you will learn to time your swing correctly for the different lengths of clubs, thus hitting the ball the optimum distance with each club. Until your game develops to the point where there is a consistent difference in the distance you stroke the ball with the various clubs, a minimum set of clubs will probably serve you best.

The irons are versatile clubs. You can hit the ball from various situations with them. You can make certain adjustments to vary the distances and trajectories of ball flight. For instance, the shot you wish to make is too far for a 7-iron, and a 5-iron will be too much club for the distance. You do not have a 6-iron. Do not try to extend the distance you normally can hit with the 7-iron. Take a 5-iron, either grip down on the handle or take a shorter swing or do both. Keep the same tempo in the swing as you would in making any golf stroke. Do not purposely slow down the swing.

If, with any specific iron, you wish to hit the ball in a higher or lower trajectory than normal for that club, you change the angle of the club face when you address the ball. Increasing the club face angle to get more loft to the shot is called "opening the face," and decreasing the angle is called "closing the face."

Playing the High Lofted Irons

When you use the high lofted irons, #7 and above, you have a short club designed for a high degree of accuracy. A swing somewhat less than the full swing is recommended for these shots. This is sensible for there is less movement involved in a three-quarter swing than in a full swing, thus a greater chance of being accurate. This motion is an extension of the half swing. No great effort need be made to increase the swing. With a purpose of stroking the ball a slightly longer distance, you will naturally take a longer swing. Some fine players use an approximate three-quarter swing (fig. 6.1) for all the full iron shots and for the wood shots.

THE WOODS

Club Selection

When you play golf on a regulation course you probably will tee off with a wood on at least fourteen of the eighteen holes. Most courses have four par 3 holes. All or some of the par 3 holes will be less than wood length. On many of the long holes your drive from the tee will be followed by using a wood if the lie of the ball and the distance warrant it. Hitting long, straight wood shots is surely one of the great pleasures of golf. It is a pleasure and a thrill to see the ball travel this long distance, and it is a great feeling to coordinate this complex movement so that the maximum clubhead speed and accuracy are attained at contact and through the contact area. In a fine wood shot the club is literally flying through the impact zone. It is important to note this. You trust that the swiftly moving clubhead will stroke the ball squarely.

Due to the size and shape of the clubhead and the slight loft of the club face, the woods are not as versatile as the irons. The driver is designed to strike the ball from a tee. Only in rare circumstances would it be used from the fairway. The lie of the ball is a more important factor than the distance in deciding whether you will use a wood and what wood you will use. Even though you are a wood distance from the green, the circumstances under which you must play the ball may necessitate your using an iron rather than a wood. The 2-wood can be used only from an exceptionally good lie on the fairway. The higher lofted woods, #4 and #5, can be used for poorer lies and shorter distances than the 2- and 3-woods. If you have only one wood in your starting set, choose the 3-wood because you can use it on the tee and from the fairway.

Distance and the Correct Purpose

Progressing to the point of stroking the ball with the woods should not be a complicated step. Your objective is to strike the ball to a more distance target than you can reach with your longest iron, but a target within your distance potential. If the objective should become hitting the ball with all one's might, complications arise: poor coordinations and muscle tensions. They are the curse of the beginner and experienced player alike.

You do not have to know muscle action to make a golf swing, but some practical knowledge about muscle action can be helpful to you. Try this experiment related to using muscles effectively and ineffectively. Extend your right arm out in front of you with your palm facing up. Bend the right elbow and touch your fingers to your shoulder. Return the arm to your side. Now extend your arm out similarly again but this time tightly tense, (contract) all the muscles of your arm. Keeping the muscles tense, try bending your elbow. This action is now difficult, if not impossible. Why? You are preventing muscles used in the motion to perform. When you relax—let go—they can perform. Tensing up as you want the arm to move is like stepping on your car's accelerator and brake at the same time.

If you try to hit the ball "hard," as far as or even farther than you can, you tend to use muscles in such a way that they resist and even "block" the intended movement. This great exertion involved in tensing up the muscles gives you the *false feeling* that this is the way to accomplish the goal of hitting the ball a long distance.

Muscular contractions of resistance plus the strong muscular contractions to overcome the resistance may make you feel more powerful, but they spell ruin for distance and accuracy of a golf stroke. As a novice or an experienced player, you can be easily misled by the "feeling" of a golf swing. When you hit a fine shot a considerable distance you are apt to think or say: "I swung so easy." That is true. You did swing easy "muscle-wise." The muscle action was synchronized. Resistant muscular contractions were avoided, and the right muscular contractions were made so the swing felt "good." After such an experience you may think: "If I can hit the ball that far swinging 'easy,' then I'll put something into the swing and really hit the ball farther." This theorizing may seem logical. But what will you put into the swing? If it is more clubhead speed, then you can expect a longer shot. If you are misled by the feeling of "muscling the ball," then you probably can expect to hit the ball a shorter distance. When the swing felt "easy," you may have been swinging with the greatest clubhead speed.

No one can tell you the correct amount or kind of muscle action and relaxation that you should have in your swing. The fine synchronization of muscle contraction and relaxation occurring throughout the golf swing is beyond human description, but this synchronization is within human achievement.

THE SWING

Addressing the Ball

1. Aim to a definite target. Be certain the target is within your distance potential.

2. Assume a comfortable position with a feeling of readiness to swing.
3. Your feet should be approximately shoulder width apart. The stance may be slightly wider for the woods than for the irons.
4. If a waggle is made in preparation for the swing, move the clubhead back low to the ground as you would in the start of the backswing.

Starting the Swing

1. The club is swung back close to the ground.
2. There is a natural give of the body and legs in the direction of the swing. The head remains in the same position as at address.
3. The feeling and effort is one of swinging the clubhead straight back away from the ball. When the clubhead reaches a certain point it will naturally swing inside the intended line of flight.
4. The feeling of starting the clubhead away from the ball should be one of ease. Do not hurry the start, lift, or "grab" the club handle to start the swing.

Top of the Swing

1. The club is swung back to a position in which the shaft is approximately horizontal.
2. The left arm remains easily extended.
3. The right elbow is pointing down and comfortably, but slightly, away from the side. Trying to keep the elbow against the side binds the swing and reduces the size of the arc.
4. The wrists are bent (cocked) so they are approximately under the shaft.

Fig. 6.2   Addressing the Ball

Fig. 6.3   Starting the Backswing

Fig. 6.4 Top of the Swing—Front View   Fig. 6.5   Top of the Swing—Side View

5. The correct grip has been maintained.
6. The body is turned so that you are looking at the ball over the left shoulder.
7. Some weight has been shifted to the right foot. For most golfers the left heel will be raised slightly to accommodate the body turn.
8. The hips and shoulders have turned. The body has maintained the same position in relation to the ball as at address. The body has turned or coiled, but it has not moved sideways.
9. The arc of the backswing was naturally and simultaneously around the body and upward.

The Downswing

1. As the swing changes direction, there should be no rush into the downswing. The swing should feel like a continuous motion, even though there is a change of direction.
2. The purpose of taking the long backswing was to get the clubhead a distance away from the ball so it can gradually accelerate in the downswing and reach its maximum speed at contact.
3. The downswing is a natural motion of "getting set" to contact the ball with a swiftly moving clubhead.
4. As a result of "getting set" and reserving the greatest clubhead speed for impact, certain actions can be noted:
   a. The left heel returns to its original position on the ground and the weight begins to shift to the left side.
   b. The arms swing downward with the left arm remaining in its extended position and the right elbow coming into the side.

Fig. 6.6 Downswing—Front View

Fig. 6.7 Downswing—Side View

c. The wrists remain in a cocked position reserving the action of the clubhead for later in the swing.

d. The body uncoils, turns in the direction of the swing.

e. These actions blend one into the other. They take their places as parts of the downswing.

5. In striking a golf ball you do *not* TRY to make the analysis described above. These actions will occur naturally with a correct purpose in swinging the club, and with practice.

Impact

1. The body is in a firm position of balance to allow the clubhead to reach its maximum speed.

2. The clubhead catches up with the hands. There is no "wrist snap" in that the clubhead passes the hands. The hands continue moving with the clubhead through the contact area.

3. Concentrate on striking the ball to a target.

4. The head remains still. It is impossible to see the clubhead strike the ball, but the idea of "watching the club strike the ball" is a good one to follow.

Follow-through

1. The clubhead swings through close to the ground. No attempt is made to hit the ball into the air.

2. The objective of the swing is to hit the ball to a distant target. This purpose and the clubhead speed determine the proper follow-through.

Fig. 6.8 Impact   Fig. 6.9 Contact   Fig. 6.10 Follow-through

If the objective is only to "hit" the ball, the chances that the follow-through will be correct are poor.

3. Good balance has been maintained throughout the swing.

4. The clubhead speed with its resultant centrifugal force exerts an outward pull reacting on the arms, body, and legs.

5. At the finish of the swing, the hips have turned along with the shoulders so you are facing the intended target. The head turns to accommodate the full finish of the swing and to see the shot result.

6. The right knee has bent and turned so it is touching or almost touching the left knee.

PRACTICE SUGGESTIONS

1. Start practice sessions with the short irons and work to the full swings with the irons and woods. Starting practice with a driver and trying to hit the ball a long distance is not recommended: there is a chance of muscle and joint strain without a warm-up; and, usually a person places too much emphasis on "hitting hard" instead of placing emphasis on developing and "grooving" a good swing which will in turn produce accurate and long golf shots.

2. As you practice, note the length of the shots. Learn distances as you practice. For instance, learn to hit the ball 75 yards, 100 yards, 130 yards, etc. This will prepare you for playing golf.

3. As you take practice swings without hitting a ball, watch the club cut through the grass. Work for a smooth, swift swing. If you wish to check the position of your head when you swing, stand so your shadow casts in front of you and watch the shadow of your head.

4. If you have difficulty with the long irons and woods, try gripping down on the handle of the club. This shorter hold on the club may give you better control and more successful shots.

SAM SNEAD

Courtesy of Wilson Sporting Goods Co.

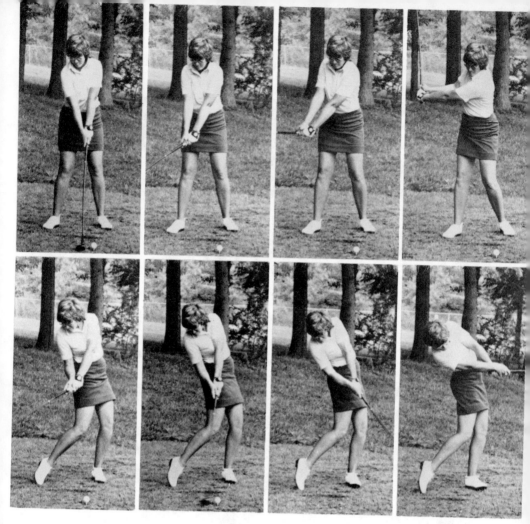

5. If you are having trouble hitting the long shots off the grass—the woods and the irons—then tee the ball and hit some shots. After you have had some success hitting the ball from a tee, then place the ball in a good lie on the turf and practice hitting off the grass. Do not have any misgivings about making the stroke easier by teeing the ball. When you are hitting your shots well, then you can try hitting the ball from various positions on the turf.

6. If you are stroking the ball from artificial turf or from hard ground, do not try to hit down and to take divots on iron shots. There is a chance of injury to the hands, wrists, and arms from the reverberation of the shock of hitting a hard surface. A divot may be the result of a good shot, but taking a divot is not a "must" for hitting good iron shots. Many fine iron shots are hit without taking divots.

7. Practice hitting all shots to a specific target.. This gives your swing the correct purpose.

Sandra Haynie, Member Advisory Staff, Dunlop, Courtesy of Golf Digest.

8. Practice the exercises for the footwork and the body turn.

9. Practice swinging the club as if it were a baseball bat. Take the golf grip and let the left arm remain easily extended during the swing. Swing the club over your right shoulder, then over your left shoulder. Through the contact area swing the club at shoulder height, waist height, and then close to the ground like the golf swing.

10. As you practice to increase the distance of your stroke, do not tighten up. Do the opposite, loosen up.

11. At times overextend yourself in practice to develop endurance of a physical and mental (concentrative) nature. After a good practice session you may well be tired. Any golfer with a low handicap knows the work involved in developing a golf game. This is one of the pleasures of golf.

The putting stroke

7

The top tournament professional golfers, men and women, shoot sub-par rounds often. The key stroke in their below-par rounds is putting. If a professional golfer were asked: "Of all the golf strokes, which one would you want at its peak during a tournament?" The answer would be unanimous: "Putting."

If par is 72 for a course, 36 strokes are allotted for distance shots to reach the putting green and 36 strokes are assigned for putting. In a round of 18 holes, all players—from the novice to the professional—can often expect to take less than 36 putts, but rarely can players expect to take less than 36 strokes to reach the putting greens. Reaching a green in the par figure allotted for a hole is commonly called either "being on in regulation" or "hitting the green." If you read that a professional player was "on in regulation" on all 18 holes or that he "hit 18 greens" you will know that he was on the putting green in the distance allotment figures on all 18 holes. When this golfer plays his first putt on each green, he is shooting for a score of 1 under par for the hole—a birdie. If he takes 1 putt on 6 of the greens and 2 putts on the other 12 greens, thereby taking a total of 30 putts and scoring six birdies and twelve pars, his total score for the round will be 66—a superb round of golf! Taking less than 36 putts and reaching the greens in near regulation figures is the way sub-par rounds are customarily scored.

It would be most unusual for a player to take 36 putts and score below par for a round, because there are few greens, if any, that a player can reach in less than regulation figures. Par 5 holes for men and par 5 and

Line up 6 balls around the cup on the practice putting green, starting at 2 feet from the hole. Putt all 6 balls into the cup, rolling them right into the center of the hole. Move back to a distance of 4 feet from the hole and attempt to sink the putts from there. Continue the same practice for longer putts.

1. Check your position addressing the ball. Are you relaxed and comfortable? Is the sole of the putter flat on the ground? Are your eyes directly above the ball? Do you have the ball lined up with the center of the club face?

2. Check your stroke. Does the putter head stay close to the ground? Are you swinging the putter approximately on the correct line? Is the stroke smooth and easy?

3. Test your progress and accuracy in putting. Are the 1- to 2-foot putts becoming almost automatic to make? Are you able to sink a greater number of long putts than formerly? When you miss a putt, does the ball come to rest very close to the hole so that the next putt is an easy "tap in".

---

par 6 holes for women can sometimes be reached in less than regulation by long hitters. If a player reaches the green of a par 5 hole in two shots or reaches the green of a par 6 hole in three shots, he or she is then putting for a score of 2 under par for the hole—an eagle. It is possible, but rare, for a player to reach the green of a par 4 hole in one stroke. The hole must be either especially short for its par or unusual conditions must exist, such as, hard ground or wind aiding the distance of the shot from the tee.

The encouraging aspects of putting are that the stroke is easy to learn and that everyone can become proficient in executing the stroke. If open torunaments in putting were held—to include amateurs, professionals, men, and women—it would not be wise to bet only on the professionals, because there are many average men and women golfers who are exceptionally skillful in putting. Your goal in putting should be to take only one or two putts per hole. You cannot become a good player until you become a consistently good putter. Putting gives you chances to score under par on certain holes and opportunities to make up for any error shots in your play from the tee to the putting green.

PUTTING—AN INDIVIDUAL STROKE

You can assert your individuality in this stroke by your choice of a putter, by your hold on the club, and by your stance. Numerous styles of putters are sold, which is proof that no one style of putter can be recommended for assured successful strokes. Some players use one putter throughout their golfing years. They would not consider changing putters even though they change woods and irons as new models are marketed. At the other extreme are the golfers who blame the club for all their putting woes and change putters frequently. Generally they never find the right club. The key factors in holding the club and addressing the ball are comfort and ease. There is one rule limitation on the stance: the U.S.G.A. rules do not allow you to putt the ball in a fashion similar to one you might use to hit a croquet ball. You cannot make a stroke on the putting green "from a stance astride, or with either foot touching, the line of putt or an extension of that line behind the ball" (Rule 35 1L). Aside from this rule you have great latitude and can adopt your own style of grip and stance. However, the expert putters do agree on and follow certain basics, and it is recommended that you do not stray too far from the following widely accepted principles.

The Grip

The reverse overlapping grip is the most widely used.

In this grip, the index finger of the left hand either overlaps the little finger of the right hand or extends down overlapping more than one finger.

The thumbs are straight down the front of the shaft.

The palms may either oppose each other or assume a more "open" position than they do in the conventional grips for the woods and irons.

The club is held with an ease and a touch for executing a delicate stroke.

The club may be held at its full length or slightly less than full length. An extremely short hold on the club is not recommended because of the long distance the club would have to be swung for long putts.

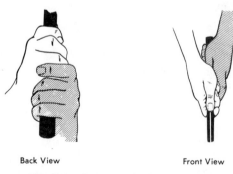

Back View   Front View

Fig. 7.1   Reverse Overlapping Grip.

The Stance

The stance may vary from a wide to a very narrow one. A medium-width, comfortable stance is recommended.

The sole of the club is placed flat on the putting surface back of the ball. With the club in this position you will naturally stand close to the ball, with your arms close to your body, and your eyes directly above the ball.

The elbows may be slightly bent. For steadiness in making the stroke, the right forearm can be placed against the right thigh.

The ball may be played in any position from a point in front of the left foot to a point out from the center of the stance. If the ball is played opposite the left foot, there may be a natural shift of the weight to the left foot in addressing the ball.

The knees are slightly bent.

Fig. 7.2   Putting Stance

The Swing

The putter head is swung back and through close to the ground in a pendulum-like motion. Naturally the length of the swing will vary with the distance of the putt. On short putts the putter will swing back and through on the intended line of roll. On long putts your feeling should be one of swinging the putter on the line, but as the swing increases in length the putter head will naturally swing inside the intended line of roll on the backswing and the follow-through. The movement is a combination of hand, wrist, and arm action. The body should remain still. It has no contribution to make to this small swing, except to provide stability. During the swing and especially the follow-through there should be a feeling of the hands moving with the putter head. The ball should not be jabbed with the clubhead while the hands are held back. Like all golf strokes, watch the putter stroke the ball. Ease is the key to good putting.

Aiming

To aim correctly you simply have the face of the club pointing to your objective. Your objective may be the hole or may be a spot on the green if you have to allow for a down and sidehill roll of the ball. When you address the ball, be certain it is lined up with the center of the club face, never toward the toe of the club. It may be helpful to momentarily place the putter head in front of the ball to line up the face with the target. In the address position turn your head to the objective while you sight and visualize the desired putt, then run your eyes back along the line through the ball and beyond it where you intend to start the putter back. Proceed to stroke the ball without unnecessary delay. Delay tends to induce tension.

Your goal in putting should be to roll the ball into the cup, but if the ball does not drop into the hole then you want it to come to rest inches or less from the hole. The adage "never up, never in" is a good one to remember. Putt the ball as far as the hole. Only then will it have a chance to drop in the cup.

Judgment Factors

In addition to judging distances to stroke the ball, you have other judgments to make. You must figure how to play a slope or undulation. You must learn to judge how easily the ball will roll over the putting surface. This is called "reading" a green. As you wait your turn to putt, try to stand near your ball, preferably in back of it. (See rules of etiquette.) When your turn comes to putt, you have already studied your line and figured any "break" (contour) of the green. As you wait, also learn from watching other putts. If you have a sidehill putt, and another player has already played a similar stroke, then you have the best information you can get for playing your stroke.

Putting greens are referred to as "fast" or "slow," depending upon how easily the ball rolls over the surface. The condition and type of grass determines how fast or slow a green will be. If the turf is thin and dried out the green will be faster than if the turf is thick and wet. There are various grasses used for putting greens. One type is a bent grass. The grain of this grass influences the role of the ball. A putt against the grain will require a firmer stroke and a putt with the grain a lighter stroke. You can make some judgment as to how fast or how slow greens will be by practicing on the practice green before you start your round, and then watching the stroke results of your companions during play.

PRACTICE SUGGESTIONS

1. Use several golf balls and start your practice with the balls about a foot away from the hole. Simply stroke the balls into the cup with little or no thought regarding how it is done. Gradually increase the distance to long putts. Let your "instinct" for aiming and judging take over. If the ball does not fall into the cup, it should come to rest very close to the hole.

2. Stroke the ball and listen for it to drop in the cup. This practice will help train you to remain calm and confident, not anxious about the result. The person who starts steering a putt immediately upon contacting the ball has only the intention of missing the putt, not of making it.

3. Practice at home on carpeting. It does not matter if the surface is different than grass. You are practicing to develop a stroke and swing.

4. When necessary, review some putting fundamentals. After the review, proceed to concentrate on sinking putts.

5. After a session of starting with short putts and working back to long distances, try a variety of putts—short, long, uphill, downhill, sidehill, and from off the apron of the greeen. Practice lining up the putts without delay. Learn to size up the situation and proceed at once to make the putt.

6. If in practice or play the putts are "rimming" the cup, with many close putts and "just misses," do not fret. You are putting well. The putts will start dropping so do not change this good stroke.

7. On sidehill putts visualize the curved path on which the ball must roll to drop into the cup. Pick out a spot on this path for your point of aim—as a bowler might do in spot bowling. Use such points as a different colored section of grass or a dead blade of grass. (A dead blade of grass may be removed, but if it is an aid in aiming, make use of it. It will not deflect the roll of the ball.)

8. Stroke the ball so it will roll smoothly over the green. The ball should not bob up and down—it should "hug" the putting surface in a forward end-over-end roll—overspin. You can easily check the roll of the ball: draw a circumference line around the ball with a colored marking pencil, place the ball in a position so the marked line is

in the perpendicular plane, and then stroke the ball and check to see if the line stays in the same plane.

9. For self-testing practice, play nine different holes of a putting course. Par would be 18 for the nine holes. Check the number of strokes you are above or below par. Some of your practice may be in match or stroke competition with another player. This practice is enjoyable, stimulating, and challenging.

10. A practice session should last at least twenty minutes. After you have had some experience in putting avoid analysis and details of action. Work on a smooth, easy, and comfortable stroke. Anyone who can swing a putter can learn to putt well. Good putting is up to you!

Courtesy of Wilson Sporting Goods Co.

BILLY CASPER

Shots requiring
special consideration

8

PLAYING FROM A BUNKER (SAND TRAP)

To add to the difficulty of golf, shallow to deep pits filled with sand are placed strategically on the course. The U.S.G.A. prefers to refer to these areas as bunkers; however, they are more often called sand traps. Creeks, lakes, and sand traps are defined as hazards, and special rules are in effect in these areas. One such rule is that you cannot ground the clubhead in the hazards, which means that you may not touch the surface of the hazard with the clubhead before taking your forward swing to hit the ball. A practice swing may be taken in a hazard provided you do NOT touch the surface of the bunker or water hazard during your swing. (See chapter 10, Rules)

The factors determining the kind of shot that should be played from the bunker are: (1) the lie of the ball in the sand; (2) the physical features of the sand trap and the area beyond the trap; and, (3) the desired distance of the shot. If the bunker is shallow and the ball is lying in a good position, you will have few or no adjustments to make. If the bunker is deep and there is overhanging turf, or if the ball is lying deep in the sand, you will have to play your shot differently than you would the usual golf shot. Here are some typical situations any golfer may encounter.

Your ball is in a shallow sand trap 225 yards from the green. The ball is lying in a good position on the sand.

1. Choose a club in which you have confidence. There is reason to believe that it will take two strokes to reach the green. You can afford to sacrifice distance in your shot from the sand trap. In general, do not risk using a club, such as a wood, for distance, and end up playing a second stroke from the trap.

2. Work your feet well down into the sand for a firm stance to maintain balance.

3. Try to contact the ball before you contact any sand. If the ball is sitting well up in the sand, you may hit the ball cleanly from the bunker so that the sand is scarcely disturbed by the clubhead. Swing to stroke the ball to your target. Do not try to lift the ball in striking it. The angle of the club face will loft the ball into the air.

Your ball is lying in a shallow sand trap adjacent to the putting green. There is no overhanging turf on the bunker. The ball is sitting well up on the sand. (Either of two shots, both relatively simple, may be played.)

1. Play a short iron shot to the green as you would play any short approach shot.

2. Putt the ball from the trap. This is an easy shot to play, and is used successfully by the novice as well as by the expert.

Your ball is lying either in a deep bunker with overhanging turf or deep in a hole in soft sand. The bunker is adjacent to the putting green (figs. 8.1 and 8.2).

Fig. 8.1   Ball in Deep Bunker.   Fig. 8.2   Wedge Shot from Bunker.

1. Use a wedge or the highest lofted iron you have. Open the club face so it points more skyward.

2. Work your feet well down into the sand for a firm stance. Play the ball in a position more opposite the left foot. If desired, take an open stance.

3. Depending upon the texture of the sand and the distance you wish to hit the ball, aim to strike the sand one to three inches back of the ball. The club face does not actually contact the ball. At impact there is a cushion of sand between the club face and the ball. The length of the swing may vary from a short swing to a full swing. Be certain you continue swinging through the sand and the ball, sweeping out sand with the ball. Make the swing smooth and continuous. Do not dig down in the sand with the clubhead, rather try to "splash" the sand out with the ball.

PLAYING HILLSIDE LIES

When you are playing a shot from a very slight, gentle slope assume a comfortable stance and play the shot just as you would any golf shot. If the hillside is steep, then you may find it necessary to make some adjustments in playing the stroke. Some players become so wrapped up in taking their stance, that taking the stance is almost all they accomplish—the shot result is often poor. Instead of following details on weight distribution, trust your instinctive sense of feel to guide you in taking a comfortable stance and in maintaining balance.

PLAYING SITUATIONS—Hole #8

Study each situation, 0-9, then plan the best way to play the shot. (You have the minimum set of 7 clubs recommended in the text)

1. Estimate the distance to the hole.
2. Determine and visualize the shot you desire.
3. Decide on the best club for the shot.
4. Are there particulars unique to the situation?

Imagine your ball in other positions and plan your strategy of play.

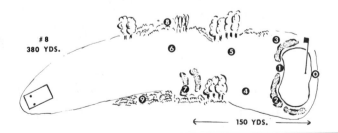

#8
380 YDS.

← —— 150 YDS. —— →

You have a sidehill-uphill lie. You must stand so one foot is higher than the other (fig. 8.3).

1. Play the ball from a position favoring the higher side of the stance. Settle in your stance so you are in balance.

2. In addressing the ball, be careful that you do not cause the ball to move. To avoid the chance of moving the ball in the address, place the clubhead farther back of the ball than you normally do, or hold the clubhead slightly above the ground.

3. On long shots aim slightly to the right of your intended target because in this situation there is a tendency to hit the ball to the left.

You have a sidehill-downhill lie (fig. 8.4).

1. Play the ball from a position favoring the higher side of the stance. Settle in your stance so you are in balance.

2. On long shots aim slightly to the left of your intended target because there is a tendency to hit the ball to the right.

3. There will be a tendency for the ball to travel in a lower trajectory, so you may choose to play the shot with a more lofted club.

Your feet are on level ground; the ball is on a level above your feet.

1. If necessary grip down on the handle of the club.

2. Aim slightly to the right because there may be a tendency to hit the ball to the left.

Your feet are on level ground; the ball is on a level below your feet.

1. Settle well down in your stance to keep your balance in swinging.

2. Aim slightly to the left because there may be a tendency to hit the ball to the right.

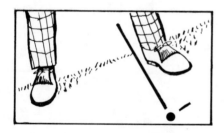

Fig. 8.3 Uphill Lie

Fig. 8.4 Downhill Lie

PLAYING FROM THE ROUGH

In the areas known as rough, conditions will vary. On some courses the rough may be no problem—you can play the ball almost as you would play it from the fairway. Problems arise when you must hit the ball from long or heavy growth.

1. When the growth of the rough is especially tall or thick, your prime objective should be to hit the ball onto an area clear of the rough. Forget any distance objective.

2. Use a club that will raise the ball sharply into the air. If necessary, open the club face. On the backswing, swing the clubhead in a more upward arc to avoid the interference of the tall grass.

3. Maintain a firm grip and keep swinging the clubhead through the ball. Do not merely chop at the ball.

4. In addressing the ball or in moving loose impediments, be careful that you do not cause the ball to move. The penalty for accidentally moving a ball in play is one stroke. (See chapter 10, General Rules #4)

PLAYING IN THE WIND

Just keeping one's balance when playing golf in a strong wind is a problem. On seaside courses in Scotland where high winds are common, it is jokingly said that golfers have trouble keeping their balance on a calm day—for without the wind, there is nothing to lean against. Generally, playing golf in the wind is more difficult than playing golf on a calm day. However, some of this difficulty is a result of trying to "fight" the wind. Players tense up trying to get distance, thereby causing the ball to be stroked poorly. When you are playing in the wind, avoid making or increasing problems by tensing up. To help keep your balance and stroke the ball more accurately, instead of taking a full swing, try taking a shorter, more controlled swing.

To check the direction the wind is blowing, note how the pennant on the flagstick is flying, or toss some blades of grass into the air and check the direction they are carried by the wind.

The wind is blowing the same direction as your desired shot.

1. Make use of the wind. When teeing off with a driver, tee your ball higher than normal, or use a more lofted wood to tee off.

2. In playing a full shot to the green consider if the wind is strong enough to carry your ball a greater distance, thus indicating the use of a shorter club.

3. If the wind is especially strong, do not try to hit high pitch shots to the putting green. Wind usually takes the backspin off the ball.

The wind is blowing toward you and in the direction opposite to that of your intended shot.

1. When teeing off, tee the ball lower for a possible lower flight, thus avoiding some wind interference.
2. The wind will decrease the distance of a shot, so select a longer club than you would generally use.
3. Do not try to hit high pitch shots into the putting green. It is too difficult to judge how much the wind will affect the ball.
4. In playing against the wind, avoid the tendency to swing harder to make up for a possible distance loss due to wind interference. Do not change your swing to "fight" the wind.

The wind is blowing across the direction of your desired shot.

1. Aim into the wind to allow for the carry of the ball in the wind direction.
2. In general, try to play lower shots that will be less affected by the wind. (See Index—Trajectory)

JULIUS BOROS

Courtesy of Wilson Sporting Goods Co.

Improving
your golf game

9

ATTITUDE AND CONCENTRATION

1. Your initial approach to the game must be that you can learn it. Then, after you have spent enough time in practice, learning to stroke the ball well, you can think positively and with confidence about your game. From resulting success you will develop a positive attitude toward each shot you play. This positive attitude which is necessary for good golf cannot be fantasy. It must be something real, based on experience.

2. Golf requires concentration. You direct your thought and attention to the golf shot to be played. Fears and anxieties of the shot results must be blocked out of your thinking. Concentration does not mean taking a long time to prepare to stroke the ball—such a practice is of little or no help and only builds up tensions. Taking a lot of time may be only a subconscious stalling, an outcome of fear. Any plan of concentration should be simple: set an objective and then proceed to attain it with little delay. Plan your stroke, come to a definite decision, visualize the shot you desire, and then proceed to execute the shot. Stroke each shot with the thought in mind that you will accomplish your goal.

3. Hitting good golf shots requires a certain amount of relaxation. Instead of attacking the game in a grim manner, try swinging the club gracefully and in good form. This is a key to stroking the ball well.

4. Good performance should be automatic. Faced with a certain shot, you will "feed" in necessary information, e.g., distance, mental picture

of shot, etc., then like the computer you will "press the button" for automatic performance. You will tell yourself *what* to do—not *how* to do it.

5. If you hit one poor shot, do not hastily decide you are "off your game." A few poorly hit shots do not necessarily make a bad round. An error shot may be a blessing in disguise—you may make a brilliant recovery from a poor shot, and that recovery will stimulate you to play an excellent round.

6. Do not label yourself negatively as: "I can't putt," "I can't aim," "I can't use my 3-wood," etc. This could lead to poor play. Also, such statements made aloud are both boring and distracting to your fellow players.

7. Accept the responsibility for the shots you play. What someone else says or does should not affect your game adversely. Do not blame anyone or any bad break for a poor shot. Keep control of your game, then you can improve it.

8. The only strategy in competition is to play your own game. Players have been known to use schemes to upset their opponents, but this is not golf.

9. Golf requires perseverance and patience. When you are "off your game" do not allow yourself to be completely disheartened. Golf has a way of leveling our egos. It is forever challenging each of us to develop a sound, consistent game.

LESSONS AND SELF-COACHING

The pursuit of skill never ends. As long as you play golf you will take golf lessons—either from a golf teacher or from yourself in the form of self-coaching. This is the experience of all golfers, even the expert tournament professionals.

You will profit most from class or private lessons if you follow certain practices.

1. Work with your instructor. You will benefit from his knowledge, experience, and observation of your swing. When you are taking lessons do not work on pet theories of your own. To do an effective job of teaching, your instructor must know what you are trying to do.

2. When you are given a cue about your swing, do not expect a miracle to happen with the next shot. The result of a shot or two is not absolute proof of the worth or worthlessness of instruction. If you hit a poor shot, do not say or think: "See, it doesn't work," or, "I can't do it your way."

3. After you receive a cue to change your swing, it may feel to you that you are following the cue and that your swing has changed drastically. For example, assume you have been swinging the club back beyond the horizontal position. The instructor asks you to take a three-quarter swing, and you take what "feels" to be that length swing. Your instructor tells you the shaft was again swung beyond the horizontal. The changes you feel do not necessarily match what actually happens in your swing.

4. In a golf class general instruction in the fundamentals and some individual coaching will be given. There is good reason for individual help—all swings do not develop the same. Remember that the coaching given another member of your class may not be useful to you.

5. Do not be disappointed and feel that you are not getting your "money's worth" if your instructor implies or says your swing looks fine and what you need is practice and play, not more instruction in swing analysis.

6. Finally, make your lessons more effective and profitable by setting up a practice program. *If you do not practice, do not expect good performance.*

Intelligent self-coaching builds your golf game; poor self-coaching destroys it. Your future golf game might be influenced most by your self-teaching.

1. If you find yourself with a persistent problem, you will probably save yourself much frustration and time if you take a lesson from a competent teacher instead of continuing to work alone.

2. There is a mass of data you can gather on the golf swings—from reading, lessons, watching expert golfers in action, and listening to other golfers. Be intelligent and discriminating in sorting this data. Is it sound? Does it apply to you? There is a bad and a good side to accumulating information: you may "jam" your brain with too much data; on the other hand, you may be enlightened by a new and different approach to the swing.

3. If you arc having trouble with a particular shot or club, do not decide that you will proceed with correcting and mastering this one problem only. If other shots are being hit well, the error may be mental. You actually prevent yourself from performing well by expecting a poor result. Put the club away and forget it. Work on strokes you are hitting well, then go back to your "problem" for short practice periods. You will achieve success and gain confidence by using this procedure.

4. You cannot avoid the experience common to all golfers—going into a slump. This may be the result of either some error in your stroke or it may be mental. Do not panic and look for gross errors in your swing. Concentrate on what to do right, not on "What am I doing wrong?" Go back to the *basics:* check your grip, stance, and address position; work on a smooth, rhythmic stroke; work on good form. Go back to the simple: practice the short approach shots and work up to longer shots. You will have success with the short shots—they are not that complicated. The chances are good you will regain your touch; besides, you will be practicing and developing a very important part of your game.

5. The hands are the connecting link with the club. They must direct, control, and transmit power. A player who has a fine sense of control with his fingers and hands will stroke the ball well. In taking a full swing to hit the ball a long distance, a player too often abandons all thought of swinging the clubhead and all sense of control of the clubhead with the hands. The hands should work together as a unit and coordinate all movements that make up the swing. *Sense the hands directing and controlling the clubhead action and transmitting power to the clubhead. Think hands and clubhead.*

6. Theories for hitting golf shots and correcting swings abound. At any given time you can go to a practice range and get "free" lessons by asking almost any player for advice. The value of these lessons can be questioned. Many golfers like to tell their "secrets of success." These tips vary from day to day. A tip that seems a miraculous cure one day is discarded the next. Do not be hasty in adopting these tips.

Correct Impact   Error—Topping

Fig. 9.1

EXAMINATION OF SOME ERROR SHOTS

Topping

A topped ball is hit above its center, thus imparting topspin to the ball. This shot may travel in the air a short distance and then dive to the ground, or the ball may just roll along the ground. In considering corrections for this error, direct your attention to club face and ball contact (fig. 9.1).

1. Ask yourself: "What am I trying to do?" If you are trying to "hit the ball into the air" or "get under the ball," then you have selected the wrong purpose to your swing. Such thoughts will lead to topping. You should not try to lift the ball into the air; remember that it's the club face that lofts the ball.

2. If you will try to hit the ball so that it will travel in a low trajectory, the clubhead should travel low through the contact area; thus the chances are good that correct club face and ball contact will be made.

3. In the address position, instead of looking at the top of the ball, watch a spot at the back of the ball where contact should be made.

4. Do not tense your shoulders and arms in the impact zone, thereby drawing the club in toward you and away from the ball.

5. If the ball is hit from a tee, sweep out the tee as you strike the ball. If the ball is hit from the grass, sweep the grass after the ball is struck. Practice swinging without a ball, keeping the clubhead low and sweeping the grass through the impact zone.

The commonly heard correction for topping is "keep your head down." At times this cue may work for you, but it is so limited in scope that the adoption of this idea only can be questionable. Can you keep your head (cranium) down and still top the ball? Of course you can, because only the clubhead tops the ball. Raising the head is more the result of, not the cause of, topping. When a ball is topped the clubhead action through the impact zone is upward. This action tends to force the head and body to move up. The body weight may not shift to the left foot, and in extreme cases, there may be a shift of weight to the right foot with the left heel raising from the ground. This strange form is the result of the erroneous effort of swinging upward. Another reason a player raises his head is that he changes his focus of attention from the execution of the shot to the shot result. Because of tension and anxiety he looks up quickly to see what happened to the ball. These are reasons why "keep your head down" is not the complete answer to the problems of striking a golf ball. When correcting topping, center your attention on the cause of the error, not on the result of the error.

Striking the Ground Before Ball Contact—"Fat" Shot

This error may be related to topping if an attempt is made to "scoop" the ball into the air. Quick, violent exertions in the impact area can also result in "fat" shots. To correct the error, discard any wrong purpose of trying to "scoop" the ball into the air and develop a smooth swing. Once a player hits several "fat" shots, especially short pitch shots, a feeling of apprehension arises when another such shot must be played. Such fears can be dispelled and the error corrected by practice on the practice range. (See chapter 5: Grip, Hand Action, and Wrist Action; also fig. 9.2.)

Fig. 9.2   Scooping Action—Incorrect Correct Hand Action.

Shanking the Ball

If shanking the ball were a common error, the population of golfers might decrease considerably. Shanking can be described as the most ornery error in golf. This shot is hit with an iron and the ball is contacted near the neck of the club, the rounded surface at the heel of the club face. When the ball is struck with this rounded surface, the ball "squirts" out to the right. The feeling the player experiences is horrendous, one of total ineffectiveness. There are fortunate golfers who have never or rarely shanked a shot. Those unfortunate players who go through periods of shanking might do better seeing a psychiatrist than seeing a golf teacher. The word "shank" is taboo in golf conversation—golfers fear that mention of the word will bring on the error! Opinions on corrections vary and volumes could be written on the subject. The following are possible corrections.

1. For all errors, go back to the simple—practice hitting short approach shots with a medium iron and work up to longer iron shots. Unless your swing is completely off, this may be your best correction—working on the positive and not fighting a fault.

2. When shanking occurs the clubhead is outside of the correct path at ball contact. Picking up the club on the backswing, extra effort at the start of the downswing, and extra effort through impact could all force the clubhead outside of the correct arc. To help keep the clubhead on the correct path at impact, place a tee in the ground be-

yond the ball outside the clubhead path. When you strike the ball, avoid hitting the tee, thereby keeping the clubhead on the correct path and making correct ball contact (fig. 9.3).

3. Check the spot on the club face where you are addressing the ball. Addressing the ball out toward the toe of the club face to allow for any error may be of temporary help.

Fig. 9.3

EXAMINATION OF DIRECTIONAL FLIGHT ERRORS

Why a golf shot travels off line to the right or left of the intended target should not be a mystery. To demonstrate how you can stroke a ball off line try this experiment using a putter. First, putt a ball to a target about five feet away. Then keeping the same stance and grip, putt a ball to the right of the target. Now stroke a ball so it will roll to the left of the original target. These is nothing complicated about this. If the ball rolled straight to the right or left, the putter face was at right angles to the clubhead path. If the ball rolled with clockwise or counter-clockwise spin, then the club face was not perpendicular to the path of the club.

If you play baseball or softball, it is probable that in batting practice you can successfully hit balls to left, center, and right fields. Depending upon the field into which you want the ball to travel, you time your swing so that the bat is facing the target at impact. It is not necessary to make any change in your stance at the plate. If you play tennis or table tennis, you can hit shots to right, center, or left courts with no difficulty. If you see your opponent out of position, at one side of the court, you may direct your shot to the opposite side of the court. You may even purposely put some side spin on the ball to deceive your opponent. You know through experience that the position of the hitting surface and the path of the striking implement through the contact area will determine the flight of the ball. This is basic information for examining errors in directional flight of the golf ball (see chap. 3, fig. 3.3).

Push and Slice

Both shots travel to the right of the intended target. In a push shot the path of the clubhead through the contact area is on a line toward the right of the target and the club face is perpendicular to this line. This produces a straight shot but off line to the right. In a slice, the path of the clubhead through contact can vary, but the club face in relation to the path is open or facing to the right of the path. In this contact the inner side of the ball is compressed, producing a horizontal, clockwise spin on the ball. As the spinning ball travels through the air, the ball will curve to the right (fig. 9.4). In considering corrections for these errors assume that the grip and stance are correct and the golf swing in general appears to be one of good form. There are no unusual or outstanding obvious distortions in swinging the club. If this is true, the error is produced by incorrect efforts in the contact area.

1. One of the main reasons for hitting to the right is trying to put something extra into the shot. Instead of swinging the club face to the square position the handle is pushed, thus changing either the path of the club, the club face, or both. Develop the feeling of swinging the clubhead *through* the contact area.

2. When you become anxious and fearful of the shot result, you tend to stop the swing of the clubhead through impact thereby leaving the club face open and looking up quickly to see the shot result. This is called "coming off the ball" and can result in hitting to the right.

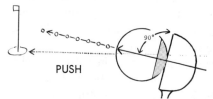

PUSH—Straight Shot to Right of Target
- Clubhead Path through Impact is on a Line Toward the Right of the Target—From Inside-Out.
- Club Face is Perpendicular to the Clubhead Path.

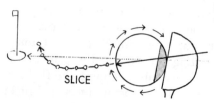

SLICE—Ball Curves to Right due to Clockwise (horizontal) Spin
- Clubhead Path through Impact can be: 1. On a Line to the Target, 2. From Outside-In, 3. From Inside-Out.
- Club Face is Pointing to the Right of the Clubhead Path.

Fig. 9.4

3. Do not try to get a straight follow-through or to "steer" the ball to the target. The result of such action is usually a hit off line to the right. Trust that the clubhead will travel in the correct path and strike the ball squarely.

4. Do not allow for any error to the right by aiming to the left of your target. You will only become more adept at the error and compound it.

5. If you have been swinging with the club face open at contact, it may "feel" that the club face is closed when you swing it to the square position. Because of this "feel" already established, you may actually have to attempt to swing the face to a closed position to reach the square position. Do not be fearful of trying to do this. If after trying the correction the ball travels straight, then you know that the face was square even if it "felt" closed to you. If the ball travels to the left then an overcorrection was made, thus producing a hook or pull.

The traditional correction for slicing has been to hit "from inside out." This may have some value for the person who has a very distorted swing with the clubhead traveling from way outside and across the intended line of flight. This is not the error of most people. Using only this cue may increase the error of hitting to the right. Recall that the path of the clubhead through the contact area should be from inside the intended line—on the intended line—and then inside again.

A closed stance is suggested frequently to correct slicing. If the player takes a closed stance and has a feeling he is aiming to the right, and then compensates for this aim by swinging the face over to direct the ball to the intended target, a closed stance would be an aid. This does not necessarily happen. Trick shot artists prove that the stance in itself does not determine ball flight. They can take any stance, stand on one foot, or even sit down and hit the ball any direction they please. The path of the clubhead through the impact area and the relation of the club face to this path determines the directional ball flight.

Pull and Hook

Both shots travel to the left of the intended target. In the pull shot the path of the clubhead through the contact area is on a line toward the left of the target and the club face is perpendicular to this line. This produces a straight shot but off line to the left. In a hook shot the path of the clubhead can vary, but the club face in relation to the clubhead path is closed or facing to the left. In this contact the outer side of the ball is compressed producing a horizontal counter-clockwise spin on the ball. As the spinning ball travels through the air, the ball will curve to the left (fig. 9.5). The errors of pulling and hooking are less common than those of pushing and slicing. Suggestions that may result in correcting the pull and hook are:

1. An incorrect grip with either one or both hands shifted more to the right than normal (right palm facing more skyward, left palm facing more toward the ground) can cause error shots to the left. (A grip in reverse of this, with either or both hands positioned more to the left, can cause error shots to the right.)

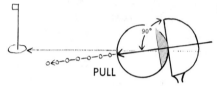

PULL—Straight Shot to Left of Target
- Clubhead Path through Impact is on a Line Toward the Left of the Target—From Outside-In.
- Club Face is Perpendicular to Clubhead Path.

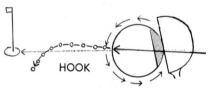

HOOK—Ball Curves to Left due to Counter-Clockwise (horizontal) Spin
- Clubhead Path through Impact can be: 1. On a Line to the Target, 2. From Inside-Out, 3. From Outside-In.
- Club Face is Pointing to the Left of the Clubhead Path.

Fig. 9.5

2. Trying to hit the ball an extra long distance and "slapping" at the ball often results in hooking the ball. The player may sense the right hand overpowering the left in the impact zone, thus closing the club face. When this error is corrected the player may sense a dramatic change in the feel of the swing. He may feel that the left hand and arm are in control of the downswing and follow-through, and that the right hand is doing little or nothing to strike the ball. He may feel that he is not "hitting the ball as hard" as he can. The feeling of striking the ball without using all one's might can produce good golf shots.

3. If there is a consistent error of pulling the ball to the left of the target, check the stance and the ball position in relation to the feet. When a player pulls a ball it may be obvious that he has turned his body too early in the impact zone. Numerous reasons could be given for this error in timing and coordination. Fear of hitting to the right may cause a player to turn on the ball to direct the ball away from an error shot to the right.

Skilled players will at times intentionally strike a ball so that it curves in flight and ends up on target. The draw shot curves in flight from right to left; the fade shot curves in flight from left to right.

PLAYING HINTS

1. Physical readiness to play golf is important. Warm up before you play: start your practice with the short swings, gradually working to the full swings. Do gentle stretching exercises for relaxation. The greatest area of tension for most people is through the neck and shoulders. Make easy movements and do stretches that will relax these areas. As you play your round of golf stay "easy" so you can use your muscles efficiently when swinging the club.

2. Study and know the golf rules. Not knowing the rules may cause you to be penalized strokes, and knowing the privileges the rules extend may prove helpful in your scoring. For example, when you drop the ball back of a water hazard, you may choose a well-kept area of grass on which to drop the ball, providing all the other provisions of the rule are followed. (See Rules—Water Hazard)

3. Play according to the rules and keep your score accurately. To do otherwise is deceiving yourself.

4. Golf should be a congenial and friendly game. When all players of your group are considerate of each other, the game is enjoyable. The golf course is not the place for a lot of talk and idle chatter. You might ask yourself: "Whose game am I most interested in?" You know that answer, and it is the same for all other golfers.

5. In your early games of golf, improving the lie of the ball on the fairway may be condoned. However, after you have developed your game, play the ball as it lies, according to the rules. Continued play of winter rules is not golf and will make stroking the ball difficult when you are required to play by the official rules.

6. Do not complain about the course you are playing. You choose the course, it does not choose you.

7. During a round of golf no instruction concerning a golf swing should be given. If you are having a bad day, accept it. Do not seek advice from another player. Also, do not offer to teach someone or to give playing tips.

8. Assume you are teeing off. There is an out of bounds along the right side of the fairway. Tee your ball toward the right side of the teeing area and aim to the center or slightly left of center of the fairway. Whenever you can, use this strategy of aiming away from trouble when teeing off.

Gene Littler, Courtesy Ram Golf Corporation.

9. The interference of a wooden tee can prevent an effective golf shot. For example, if you tee off with a lofted iron the tee and the ball might be contacted simultaneously (fig. 9.6). This contact can deflect or slow down the clubhead. When you tee off with an iron, use a broken tee that barely goes into the ground. Should the clubhead strike the tee, it will fly out of the ground with the hit and offer no resistance. Whenever you do use a long wooden tee in hard ground, loosen the turf around the tee, as you place the tee into the ground.

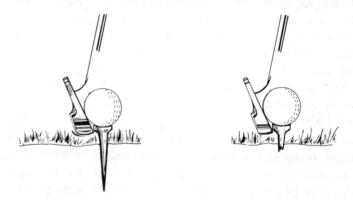

Fig. 9.6

10. To avoid tension, do not overrespond to a situation. For example, you see your ball roll into a distant sand trap. Do not react immediately in concern over playing the next shot. Practice self-discipline in thought control. When you reach the sand trap, size up the situation, plan the shot, and play it.

11. When you play golf choose the correct club for a shot by considering:

   a. The *lie* of the ball on the ground.

   b. The *distance* you want to strike the ball.

   c. The *situation*, such as whether you have to hit the ball in a high or a low trajectory, etc.

   d. The course *conditions*, such as wind directions; wet, soft, or dried out turf; etc.

   e. Your *skill* with the different clubs. If there is a choice between clubs, choose the club in which you have the most confidence.

12. Learn different distances to the green by spotting various objects, such as trees, bushes, sand traps. Learn the breaks of the greens. Figure out

and remember the most advantageous ways to play each hole. Adjust your game to the course you are playing. For example, do not try to hit pitch shots to hard greens. When the greens will not hold pitch shots and it is not necessary to loft the ball into the air, hit low run-up shots.

13. If the ball is sitting in a difficult position—on thin, sparse grass or on bare ground, take a practice swing over a spot similar in nature (if such a spot is near your ball). You have then faced the situation and are less apt to be concerned about hitting from a poor lie.

14. Do not hesitate to play a safe shot when a daring one may get you into trouble. If playing a safe shot costs you an extra stroke, there is always a chance of making up the stroke with a one-putt green.

15. Play your own game of golf. If your distance limit for a 7-iron is 120 yards, do not be challenged to hit a 7-iron 140 yards because a member of your foursome can do so. Your objective is to score well, not to hit a shot a certain distance.

16. Keep a record of your putts on the score card. In a corner of the scoring square for each hole, place a number indicating putts for the hole.

17. Take time to study your game after a round. Where did you use poor judgment in playing a shot? How many putts did you take? How many times was your approach shot to the green short of the hole? How many times was your first putt short of the hole? What part of your game needs improvement? What shots need the most practice?

Essential knowledge

10

If you are a novice you cannot expect to hit the ball like the experienced player, but you can put yourself in his class in some respects. You can gain knowledge of the game and practice correct procedures of conduct. You can become "well-informed." Supplement the following information by studying the official rule book and other golf books, and by carefully observing experienced players on the course. Be willing and ready to learn, and you will be a welcome member of any golfing group.

ETIQUETTE

The rules of etiquette are not strict formalities that complicate play. They simplify and enhance the game. Observance of these rules makes it possible to play better golf and enjoy the game more, to keep the course in good playing condition, and to allow more people to play golf by speeding up play.

Playing good golf requires concentration. Etiquette and good sportsmanship thus require that you respect and do not distract the player making a stroke. Always stand quietly and out of range of the player when he is addressing the ball or taking a stroke. Do not stand directly behind the ball or directly behind the hole.

Care of the Golf Course

1. Replace any divot and press it firmly in place. Avoid taking divots with practice swings.

2. Walk carefully on the putting green to avoid marring the surface. Do not step or stand at the edge of the hole (cup).

3. Do not drop or throw the flagstick on the green.

4. If you use a golf cart, keep it well away from the apron of the putting green.

5. Repair ball marks on the putting green. A golf tee can be used, but a better device is a fork-like metal tool—these are available at a nominal cost. Lift up and press back the grass around the pit mark leaving a level surface.

6. When you lift your ball from the wrong putting green, drop it well off that green to avoid taking a chance of damaging the apron as you stroke the ball.

7. When leaving a bunker, smooth out the surface so that its condition is as good as or better than when you entered it.

8. Do not discard any litter on the course. Do your part in maintaining the beauty of the golf course.

Playing Without Delay

1. When you pay your green fee, remember you are one of many paying for the privilege of playing on the course.

2. Be ready to play. Have a knowledge of safety, etiquette, and rules and possess basic skills in the strokes.

3. You will need your own set of clubs, golf bag, balls, and tees. Do not borrow clubs from another player. Carry your own golf bag. Do not be burdened with extra items such as purses and sweaters. Place them in the golf bag or check them at the pro shop.

4. Identify your ball before starting play. Check to see that you are not playing the same make and ball number as another player in your group. When your ball is in play, as on the fairway, do not pick up the ball for identification. Simply look around it and check the make and number. If it appears that a player in the distance is going to play your ball by mistake, call "fore" and wave to him.

5. Avoid delaying play by taking numerous practice swings.

6. Be ready to take your stroke when it is your turn. It is possible to plan ahead for some strokes. (See chap. 7—Putting)

7. Any instruction on the course should be incidental. There should not be any delay because one person is attempting to teach another.

8. When you hit a ball, spot its position carefully. Spot its position in relation to some stationary object so you can walk directly to it. Watch

the stroke results of other players in your group so you can help in any search for a ball.

9. If you, as a novice, find yourself in some difficult situation, e.g., unable to hit from a deep bunker after making several attempts, pick up the ball and drop it out of the bunker. Your scores for your early games of golf are not so important that they merit your delaying the play of others.

10. When your ball is on the wrong fairway, permit players playing that hole to have the right of way. Some courses have a local rule allowing you to lift the ball from the wrong fairway and drop it in the correct fairway. Safety and speeding up play make this an acceptable local rule.

11. If your group is delaying play by failing to keep its place, losing more than one clear hole on the players in front, invite the following group to pass. In turn, if you are extended this courtesy, express your appreciation.

12. When someone in your group is searching for his ball, help in the search. Invite following players to play through.

13. At some golf courses on par 3 holes, signs are posted directing golfers who have reached the putting green to invite players of the following group to hit their tee shots. When you follow this procedure, be certain you do not stand in line with the flagstick. Stand behind the green and off the putting surface. Standing in this position you will not disturb the players shooting onto the green, and you will be relatively safe. However, do watch the shots of the players in case someone overshoots the green. After the players have hit their tee shots, your foursome proceeds to putt out.

14. In match play and in recreational play golfers often concede putts of 8 to 10 inches or less to their playing companions. For example, Player A plays his third stroke and his ball comes to rest 5 inches from the hole. A playing companion may say, "That's good," pick up the ball, and toss it back to Player A. Player A scores a 4 on the hole. The time required for putting out is thus saved.

15. In recreational golf strict adherence to the rule requiring the ball farthest from the hole to be played first is being relaxed. In the interests of faster play there is justification for this relaxation of the rule. Examples: (a) Three people of a foursome are on the putting green. The fourth player, A, is shooting from a sand trap adjacent to the green. He hits a poor shot to the far side of the green, and his ball is farthest from the hole. It will take time for Player A to rake the trap and then walk to his ball. Instead of waiting for A to play

first, one or more of the other players is probably ready to putt and should proceed to do so. (b) You are ready to play your ball from the left side of the fairway, 150 yards from the hole. Your playing companion, B, is searching for his ball in the right rough, 160 yards from the hole. Since you are ready, it is acceptable for you to go ahead and play your shot, even though you are not away. After you play your stroke you may wish to walk over and help Player B in search for his ball. Many players follow these and similar procedures for the sake of speeding up play.

On the Putting Green

1. Place golf bag or cart well off of and on the side of the green nearest the next tee.

2. Whether a ball be on or off the putting green, the rules state that the ball farthest from the hole be played. The trend in recreational play is to allow golfers off the putting surface—whether or not they are farthest from the hole—to play first. This practice can save time because the possible necessity of alternately attending the flagstick or leaving the flagstick unattended is eliminated.

3. Do not step or stand in any line of play. Do not allow your shadow to be cast in someone's line of play.

4. Mark and lift your ball when requested to do so. To mark your ball's position, place a small coin or marker behind the ball and then lift the ball. If your ball is in a direct line of play, measure the necessary lengths of the putter head to one side of the line and place the marker at this spot. In stroke play the U.S.G.A. recommends that the ball nearer the hole be played, rather than marked and lifted, provided subsequent play of a fellow competitor is not affected. In stroke play a player has the option of either marking or playing his ball. If in playing the ball you have to stand in another player's line of putt, mark and lift your ball, do NOT take your stance in another player's line of putt. This option of "continuous putting" (instead of marking balls lying near the cup) helps speed up play on the course.

5. When holding the flagstick, stand to one side of the hole and hold both the stick and the pennant. The stick should be held in the hole until removal is necessary. Be certain you stand so that your shadow is not cast across the line of play. After removal of the flagstick, lay it down out of play. When all players are on the putting green or close to it, a player whose ball lies close to the hole generally offers to attend the flagstick.

6. When all players have holed out, replace the flagstick, leave the green immediately, and proceed to the next tee. There are safety reasons for this admonition as well as other obvious reasons. Do not stand on the green after completion of play either to review play of the hole or to mark your scores on the score card.

In the Bunker (Sand Trap)

1. Leave the bag or cart well outside the edge of the bunker.
2. Enter the bunker at the lowest bank and take the shortest route to the ball.
3. Do not enter or stand in a bunker when another player is playing from it.
4. On leaving the bunker, rake or in some manner smooth out all footprints and marks which you have made.

RULES

This is a summary of certain rules. This knowledge together with the rules of etiquette will enable you to play golf properly. However, this digest of rules is no substitute for the official rules.*

Types of Competition

Some rules differ for the two types of competition, *stroke play* and *match play*. Most golf played is stroke play. In this competition the winner is the person with the lowest score for the stipulated number of rounds, usually four rounds, a total of 72 holes. In case players are tied for the low score at the end of the tournament, the U.S.G.A. recommends that these players play another 18-hole round to determine the winner. The terms "competitor" and "fellow competitor" are used to describe the players in stroke play.

Match play competition is based on scores for each hole, not total score for a round. In a match a person competes against only one other player, his opponent. They play until one person is more holes ahead than there are holes remaining to be played in the match. If the match is tied at the end of a round, the players continue play until one player wins a hole. Match play is an elimination type tournament, so in the final round there are only two players remaining to compete for the championship.

*The official rules may be obtained from your local golf club or from the U.S.G.A., Far Hills, New Jersey 07931.

Match Play Score Card

Assume that at the end of nine holes Bill is 1 hole up on Joe. Hole #10 is tied or *halved*. Bill remains 1 up. Joe wins #11. The match is *all square*. Joe wins #12 and #13. Joe is 2 up. Hole #14 is halved. Joe wins #15. Joe is *dormie* 3. A player is dormie when he is the same number of holes up as there are holes remaining to be played. Hole #16 is halved. Joe wins the match, 3 holes up with 2 remaining, or simply 3 and 2 (3-2).

HOLE NO.	10	11	12	13	14	15	16	17	18
Bill (1 up)	5	5	4	7	4	4	4	—	
	o	−	−	−	o	−	o		
Joe (1 down)	5	3	3	5	4	3	4	—	
	o	+	+	+	o	+	o		

Fig. 10.1   Match Play Card

Rules for Teeing Off

1. Play is started on each hole by teeing the ball within the limits of the teeing area. This area is bounded in front by two tee markers and extends two club lengths back of the markers.

2. If in addressing the ball you accidentally knock it off the tee, you may replace it without penalty.

3. Honor, the privilege of teeing first, is decided by lot on the first tee. After the first hole, the honor is decided by scores on the previous hole. The person with the lowest score plays first and the others follow according to scores. If players have the same scores then the player who had the honor previously continues to tee ahead of other players.

General Rules

1. After teeing off you continue striking the ball until you hole out. The ball should be played as it lies and not be touched except to strike it, unless situations or rules require or allow you to do otherwise.

2. You play in turn so the ball farthest from the hole is played first. (Exception: Stroke play, "continuous putting" on green—see Etiquette—Putting Green. Also, other exceptions may be made in stroke play to speed up play.)

3. Any attempt to hit the ball is counted as a stroke, whether or not the ball is struck.

4. If you accidentally move the ball in play or cause it to move, this counts as a stroke. (Exception, Rule 35 1b—If you move loose impediments on the putting green and the ball is moved, you may replace the ball without penalty.)

5. If such loose impediments as fallen leaves and pebbles interfere with your play of the ball, you may move them, but they may not be moved from a hazard.

6. When the ball is in play, you cannot press or stamp down the ground near the ball or break or bend anything growing.

7. If your ball lies within two club lengths of an immovable obstruction, such as a ball washer, bench, or protective screen, you may lift the ball and drop it with no penalty. (See #8 following)

8. To drop a ball, stand facing the hole and drop the ball back over your shoulder. The ball must not be dropped nearer the hole.

9. If your ball comes to rest on the wrong putting green, you must lift the ball and drop it off the green, without penalty.

10. If your ball lies in casual water, ground under repair, or in a hole made by a burrowing animal, or if any of these conditions interfere with your stance or the area of your intended swing, you may lift the ball and drop it without penalty. If casual water interferes with your play on the putting green, after lifting the ball you place the ball free of the water rather than drop it. The ball must not be placed nearer the hole.

11. You may ask only your caddie, partner, or partner's caddie for advice regarding the playing of a stroke.

12. If another player's ball interferes with your play, you may request that he mark and lift the ball.

13. There is some difference in the penalties for the breach of a rule. (Refer to the official rule book.) The general penalty for breaking a rule is two strokes in stroke play and loss of a hole in match play. (See #5 and #6 above) If you remove loose impediments from a hazard or stamp down the grass back of the ball in play, it will cost you two strokes in stroke play, and you will immediately lose the hole in match play.

14. The score card should be checked for local rules and interpretations which apply to the course being played.

Rules for the Putting Green

1. When playing your ball on the putting green, request that the flagstick be attended or removed from the hole. The penalty for your ball striking the flagstick is two strokes in stroke play and loss of hole in match play.

2. In stroke play, when you play your ball on the putting green and your ball strikes a fellow competitor's ball, also on the putting green, the

penalty is two strokes. If this impact moves the fellow competitor's ball, he must replace it.

3. In match play, if your ball strikes your opponent's ball there is no penalty. Your opponent has the option of replacing his ball or leaving it where it comes to rest.

Rules for Hazards

1. By U.S.G.A. definition there are two types of hazards: bunkers and water hazards. A bunker usually is a depressed area of bare ground covered with sand, frequently called a sand trap. Grass-covered area surrounding the bunker is not part of the hazard. The grass-covered area or any dry ground surrounding a water hazard may be part of the hazard. Local rules will determine the limits of water hazards.

2. Loose impediments may not be moved from a hazard.

3. Man-made objects, such as a rake, may be moved.

4. In addressing the ball in a hazard, you may not ground the club. You may not touch the surface of the hazard with the clubhead before taking your forward swing to strike the ball.

5. If you lose a ball in a water hazard or find it impossible to play the ball from the hazard you may: (A) drop a ball, under penalty of one stroke, at the spot from which the original ball was played; if the original ball was played from the tee, the ball may be teed anywhere in the teeing area; or, (B) drop a ball, under penalty of one stroke, any distance behind the hazard, keeping the spot at which the ball last crossed the margin of the hazard between you and the hole. In situation A, figure 10.2, it is to your advantage to tee the ball again. In situation B, figure 10.2, you would lose too much yardage if you played again from the tee. Therefore you would usually drop a ball any distance back of the hazard, keeping the spot at which the ball last crossed the margin of the hazard between you and the hole. (Note line on which to drop ball.)

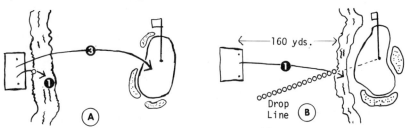

Fig. 10.2 Water Hazard

6. For a lateral water hazard you may play your next stroke in accordance with (A) or (B) in #5 above; or, (C) under penalty of one stroke, you may drop a ball within two club lengths of either side of the hazard, opposite the point where the ball last crossed the margin of the hazard, but not nearer the hole. (See fig. 10.3. Option A, drop ball at X. Option B, drop ball on line indicated. Option C, drop ball within 2 club lengths of either side of the hazard.)

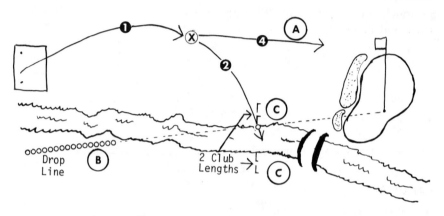

Fig. 10.3   Lateral Water Hazard

Ball Out of Bounds, Lost, or Unplayable

1. A ball is out of bounds when it lies on ground on which play is prohibited. The area is usually marked by a fence or out of bounds stakes.
2. You are allowed five minutes to search for a ball. After that time the ball is deemed lost.
3. You are the sole judge as to when your ball is unplayable.
4. If a ball is out of bounds, is lost outside a water hazard, or is deemed unplayable, the penalty is loss of distance and one stroke. The player must play his next stroke at the spot from which the original ball was played and add one penalty stroke. (See #5)
5. If the ball is unplayable, there is an optional rule. Under a penalty of one stroke the ball may be dropped either within 2 club lengths of the unplayable position but not nearer the hole; or the ball may be dropped any distance behind the point where the ball lay, keeping that point between yourself and the hole.
6. When you hit a ball that you think might be out of bounds or might be lost outside a water hazard, to save time you may at once play a provisional ball. If the original ball is playable, you play it and pick up

the provisional ball. If the original ball is out of bounds or lost, then you continue play with the provisional ball. The penalty (see #4) applies.

Stroke and Distance Rule (See fig. 10.4)

A player drives out of bounds (1). He tees another ball, adds a penalty stroke and shoots 3 from the tee. From the fairway he shoots his fourth shot into the rough and loses the ball. He drops a ball at spot (X), adds a penalty stroke and shoots stroke 6.

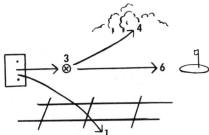

Fig. 10.4   Stroke and Distance Rule

HANDICAPS

A handicap is a number representing approximately the strokes a player shoots over par for a round. For instance, if a player has a handicap of 2, he is an excellent golfer; if he has a handicap of 25, he is a novice. A player who has a handicap of 0 averages near par and is called a scratch golfer.

To establish a handicap* a given number of rounds are played, usually 20. Score cards are turned in to the golf club or association and the handicap is figured from the 10 lowest scores of the 20.

Handicaps are used to equalize competitive play. In an 18-hole stroke play handicap event, a net score is computed for each player by subtracting his handicap from the actual (gross) score. The player with the low net score is the winner.

In match play the player with the higher handicap is allowed to subtract from his score on certain holes. For example, two opponents have handicaps of 7 and 4. The player with the 7 handicap subtracts one stroke from each of his scores on the three holes with a handicap rating of 1, 2, and 3. On the score card shown in the text, the three holes rated most difficult are #6, #14, and #9 for men, and #3, #17, and #5 for women. The player with the handicap of 4 spots the 7 handicapper one stroke on each of these holes, if the full handicap difference is allowed.

*For detailed information on handicapping and tournaments write the U.S.G.A. for *Golf Committee Manual* and *U.S.G.A. Handicap System.*

Honest and up-to-date handicaps make competition between players of unequal ability possible and enjoyable.

SELECTION OF EQUIPMENT AND ACCESSORIES

The amount of money you wish to invest in golf will determine your selection of equipment and accessories. Your initial investment can be a small one or a considerable one. Used sets of clubs and used golf balls are available, and minimum sets of new clubs and new balls are marketed at reasonable prices. A variety of new, high quality matched sets of clubs offer a wide selection to the person wishing to make a substantial investment in clubs. Generally the more expensive clubs will have more "feel." Higher quality material is used in their construction, and the time is taken to match the shafts and clubheads to insure better balance. Whether the clubs be moderately priced or expensive, it is important that they fit you. If you buy clubs from a trained, experienced golf professional or salesperson, you can expect to be fitted with the correct clubs.

Because of the differences in height, strength, and hand size between men and women, men's clubs are longer, have stronger and stiffer shafts, have larger grips, and are heavier. The average golfer will find the medium shaft best suits his needs. The person with above average power and strength might find a shaft stiffer than medium better, while a person with average or less strength and power may be helped by a more flexible shaft. The weight of clubs can vary considerably. An accepted concept in fitting clubs is to consider the swing weight of the clubs. Simply stated, swing weight is a measurement of the clubhead weight in proportion to the shaft and grip weight. This weight is given by letter and number. The swing weight of women's clubs ranges from C-0 to C-9. C-0 to C-2 is a light club, C-3 to C-6 is a medium club and C-7 to C-9 is a heavier club. Swing weights of D-0 to D-1 are light clubs for most men, D-2 and D-3 medium, and D-4 to D-6 heavy. A special scale is used to measure swing weight. There is nothing on the club to indicate the total weight or the swing weight of a club. A golf professional can check the overall and swing weight of clubs for you.

The golf bag you select will probably depend on the number of clubs you will carry and whether you will carry your clubs and bag on your shoulder or pull them on a cart. Hand golf carts to carry equipment are popular accessory items. Hand carts and motorized carts are available for rental at most courses. Certain exclusive golf clubs require players to either rent a motorized cart or hire a caddie. For people who could not otherwise play golf because of the walking limitations, the motorized carts have their points. However, the golf purists criticize the use of carts by players able to walk the course.

Wearing either a golf glove on the left hand or gloves on both hands will prevent blisters and callouses from forming on the hands, and may also help in holding the club. You will need to wear comfortable, flat-heeled oxfords. Golf shoes with spikes are preferred, for these will help you maintain balance in swinging and also will make walking on the course easier. Golf gloves and golf shoes are not absolutely necessary for your golf, but they are both recommended. Hats or visors for protection from the sun are also recommended.

Comfortable and appropriate sports clothes should be worn for golf. Complete lines of attractive golf clothes for men and women are sold in many stores, including golf shops at courses.

YOU AND THE GAME OF GOLF

Are You Ready to Attempt Play on the Course?

1. Have you developed some consistency in hitting the ball with the full swing? Do you know the distances you can get with the various clubs?

2. Have you practiced hitting different distances with the medium and short irons? Have you learned how much to "choke up" on the grip and how much swing to take for given distances?

3. Have you practiced putting so that in most longer putts of 25 feet or more you can hole out in 2 putts? Are you able to sink many putts of 1 to 2 feet in length?

4. Have you carefully studied and learned the safety precautions, etiquette, and the rules? Are you willing to watch the conduct of the experienced golfer and to learn from these observations?

Tips for Your Early Experience on the Course

1. If available, play a course consisting of short holes. If you play a full-length course, plan to play less than 18 holes, at a time when the course is not crowded.

2. If possible, have an experienced golfer guide you in correct conduct.

3. You will most likely take more strokes than the experienced golfer. Be willing to make up this time by walking rapidly between shots.

4. Don't be concerned with your scores. Become oriented to the course and follow correct procedure.

5. If you are in a difficult situation, and you may hold up play, consider possible solutions. For instance, finding it impossible to hit from deep rough—pick up your ball, toss it into the fairway and continue play;

taking many putts on the green—pick up your ball and discontinue play of this hole.

6. Golf is a complicated game. Be patient. Consider other players. With experience, study, and practice you will soon be playing golf as it should be played.

Golf Conduct

The test of a player is: Does he really play golf? One might think this a ridiculous question. However, golfing authorities are becoming increasingly critical of and concerned with present playing practices. Some people play under the guise: "I play for the fun of it." They do not choose to meet the challenges of the game by playing according to the rules; they have little or no consideration for either their fellow players or the golf course. Although in the minority, their number is great enough to detract from the game and their actions deserve censure. It is hoped that you who have read this text will make some contribution to correcting these poor practices and to preserving the fine traditions of the game.

THE GOLFER'S CODE

Meet the challenges of the game. Play by the rules. The rules are self-enforced.

Be aware of sharing the course with other players. Realize the importance of keeping your place on the course so as not to hold up the play of golfers following.

Follow practices that will help keep the course in the best possible condition.

Observe the safety precautions and the etiquette to the finest degree, thereby making play most enjoyable for yourself and for all players.

May your participation in this fine pastime be one of success and pleasure. May your participation and actions show your appreciation of the course and contribute to the recreation and pleasure of all golfers.

Glossary of terms

Ace. A hole in one.

Addressing the ball. Taking the stance and grounding the club, except that in a hazard a player has addressed the ball when he has taken his stance.

All square. A term used in match play to indicate that the match is tied.

Approach shot. A stroke played to the putting green.

Apron. The area surrounding the putting green.

Away. The ball lying farthest from the hole.

Backspin. A reverse spin of the ball in the vertical plane.

Banana ball. A slice.

Barranca. A deep ravine. (Spanish)

Bite. The backspin on the ball causing it to stop upon landing on the ground.

Birdie. A score of one under par for a hole.

Bogey. Commonly used to describe a score of one over par for a hole.

Brassie. The 2-wood.

Break of green. The slant or slope of the putting green.

Bunker. Usually a depressed area covered with sand, commonly called a sand trap.

Caddie. A person who carries the clubs and otherwise assists a player as the rules provide.

Casual water. A temporary accumulation of water not recognized as a hazard.

Chip shot. A short, low shot played to the putting green. Also called a run-up shot.

Cup. Term commonly used for the hole on the putting green.

Curtis Cup Matches. International team matches between women amateurs of Great Britain and the United States.

Divot. A piece of turf cut or displaced in making a stroke. Should be replaced and pressed down.

Dogleg. A hole in which the fairway curves to the right or left.

Dormie. A term used in match play. A player is dormie when he is as many holes up as there are holes remaining to be played.

Double bogey. A term in common use to describe a score of two over par for a hole.

Double eagle. A score of three under par for a hole.

Draw. A shot that curves slightly in flight from right to left.

Driver. The 1-wood.

Dub. An unskilled golfer; or, to hit a poor shot.

Duffer. A player with poor skill.

Eagle. A score of two under par for a hole.

Explosion shot. A shot played from a sand trap. An attempt is made to swing the club through the sand well back of the ball.

Fade. A shot that curves slightly in flight from left to right.

Fairway. The mowed grassy area between the tee and putting green.

Fat shot. A shot in which the ground is struck before contacting the ball, usually resulting in a poor shot.

Fellow competitor. The person with whom you play in stroke play.

Flagstick. The marker which indicates location of the hole.

Flat swing. A swing in which the club is swung in a low arc. At the top of the backswing the club shaft is lower than the usual orthodox swing.

Flub. A poorly hit shot; or, to hit a poor shot.

Fore!. A warning cry to anyone who might be endangered by a golf shot.

Foursome. Four players playing together who may or may not be engaged in a match.

Frog hair. The grass surrounding the putting green.

Gross score. The actual total score for a round.

Ground under repair. Staked or lined area on which work is being done. A ball coming to rest in area may be lifted and dropped in accordance with rules.

Grounding the club. Placing the sole of the club on the ground in preparation for making the stroke.

Halved or halving a hole. In match play, to tie a hole.

Handicap. The approximate number of strokes one shoots over par, or the allowance of strokes to equalize players of different ability.

Hazard. By U.S.G.A. definition, bunkers and water hazards.

High handicapper. A player who shoots many strokes over par, an unskilled player.

Hole. (1) the receptacle on the putting green 4¼ inches in diameter and at least 4 inches deep; (2) one unit or division of the course.

Hole high. The ball is in a position as far as the hole but off to either side of it.

Hole out. To complete the play of a hole.

Hook. A ball that curves in flight to the left due to a horizontal, counterclockwise spin on the ball.

Honor. The privilege of hitting first from the tee.

In 9. The second 9 holes of an 18-hole course.

L.P.G.A. Ladies Professional Golf Association of America.

Lateral Water Hazard. A water hazard running approximately parallel to the line of play.

Lie. The position of the ball on the ground.

Loft of club. The angle of pitch of the club face.

Loose impediments. Objects such as dead grass and fallen leaves, pebbles, worms, fallen twigs, etc.

Low handicapper. A skilled golfer who shoots near par.

Mashie. The 5-iron.

Match play. Competition based on scores for each hole rather than total score.

Medal play. More commonly called stroke play. Competition by total score.

Medalist. The player with the lowest score for a qualifying round of a match play tournament.

Mid-iron. The 2-iron.

Mixed foursome. A group of four players made up of two women and two men.

Mulligan. An illegal practice of taking a second drive from the first tee without penalty if the first shot is a poor one.

Nassau scoring system. A system of scoring allowing one point to the winner of each 9 holes and one point for the match.

Net score. A score resulting from subtraction of the handicap from the gross score.

Niblick. The 9-iron.

Obstruction. An artificial object on the course which may be movable or fixed.

Open tournament. A competitive event in which both amateurs and professionals play, such as the United States National Open and the British Open.

Opponent. The player opposing you in a match.

Out 9. The first 9 holes of an 18-hole course.

Out of Bounds. Ground on which play is prohibited, usually marked by out of bounds stakes or fences.

P.G.A. Men's Professional Golf Association.

Par. An arbitrary standard of scoring excellence based on the length of a hole allowing two putts on the putting green.

Pin high. Same as hole high.

Pitch shot. A shot that travels in a high trajectory played to the putting green.

Press. Attempting to hit the ball beyond one's normal power.

Pronation. An anatomical term to describe the turning of the hand and forearm inward. Supination is the opposite action in which the hand and forearm are turned out so the palm is facing up.

Provisional ball. A second ball played in case the first ball is or is thought to be lost outside a water hazard or out of bounds.

Pull. A shot that travels to the left of the intended line.

Push. A shot that travels in a straight line, but to the right of the intended target.

Rough. The areas bordering the fairway in which the grass, weeds, etc., are allowed to grow freely.

Royal and Ancient Golf Club of St. Andrews, Scotland. The governing body for mens' golf in Great Britain.

Rub of the green. An unpredictable happening to the ball when the ball in motion or at rest is stopped or deflected by an outside agency.

Ryder Cup Matches. Men's professional team matches between Great Britain and the United States.

Sand trap. The term commonly applied to a bunker.

Scotch foursome. A foursome of players in which two teams compete. Each team uses only one ball and the players alternate striking the ball.

Scratch player. A player who has a handicap of 0, shooting consistently near par.

Slice. A shot that curves in flight to the right, caused by the ball spinning in a horizontal, clockwise manner.

Spoon. The 3-wood.

Stance. The position of the feet in addressing the ball.

Stroke play. Competition by total strokes.

Stymie. To have another player's golf ball or some object blocking one's line of play—to be stymied. Also an obsolete rule of golf.

Summer rules. The ball must be played as it lies on the fairway, except as otherwise provided by the U.S.G.A. rules.

Tee. The starting place for a hole; or, the peg on which the ball is placed for driving.

Tee markers. The markers placed on the tee to indicate the forward limits of the teeing area.

Texas wedge. A name applied to the putter when it is used to play any shot from off the putting green.

Through the green. This is the whole of the course, except the teeing ground and putting green of the hole being played and all hazards.

Underclubbing. Using a club that will not give enough distance for the desired shot. For instance, using a 7-iron when a 6-iron or 5-iron should be used—a more common error than overclubbing.

Upright swing. A swing in which the club is swung high into the air on the backswing and follow-through. The opposite of a flat swing.

U.S.G.A. The United States Golf Association—governing body of golf in the U.S.A.

Walker Cup Matches. Matches between men amateurs of Great Britain and the United States.

Whiff. To swing at the ball and miss it completely—to fan.

Winter rules. Special local rules which permit the ball to be moved to a better lie on the fairway; also called "preferred lies."

Appendix:
Questions and answers

If you can correctly answer all of the questions in this test, your knowledge of golf is probably above that of the average person playing the game. The test covers etiquette, safety, definitions, and selected rules. The questions on rules are arranged so that you can easily check them in the current rule book. The rule number is listed and questions relating to that rule follow. It is recommended that you study the complete qualifications of each rule and the rules not covered in the test.

The test consists of 140 TRUE-FALSE questions and 60 questions requiring written answers. The answer key to the TRUE-FALSE questions follow the test. The answers to the essay type questions can be found in the text.

TRUE-FALSE. If the statement is TRUE, encircle the letter T. If the statement is FALSE, or partially FALSE, encircle the letter F.

I. ETIQUETTE

T   F   1. Your golf course etiquette indicates your consideration for other players on the course.

T   F   2. After playing a stroke from a sand trap, a player should smooth out all marks he made in the sand.

T   F   3. Players should record their scores on the scorecard before leaving the putting green.

T   F   4. No player should play a stroke until the group ahead is out of range.

T   F   5. If a group of players fails to keep its place on the course and loses more than one clear hole on the group in front, the slow group should allow the following group to play through.

T   F   6. Players while looking for a lost ball have signalled the group following them to pass. Before the second group has passed, however, the ball is found. The first group should hurry and immediately continue play.

T   F   7. When attending the flagstick for a fellow competitor, the flagstick should be removed from the hole and held in a position directly back of the cup.

T   F   8. All divots should be replaced and pressed firmly in place.

T   F   9. Before you tee off from the first tee, be sure to take about six practice swings on the tee in order to warm up properly.

T F 10. Before teeing off from the first tee, members of a foursome should check the names and numbers of the golf balls they intend to use.

T F 11. When playing golf, concentrate on your own game. Do not watch the shots of other players in your group.

T F 12. The approved and best way to identify your ball in play is to pick the ball up from the ground and check the name and number.

T F 13. When your ball is on or near the putting green, place your golf bag on the apron and well off the green preferably on the side of the green nearest the next tee. Do not leave your golf bag at the front of the green.

T F 14. It is good practice and improves your game to take several practice swings before each golf shot you must play.

T F 15. When you hold the flagstick for another player, always stand to the left side of the hole and hold the flagstick and pennant with your right hand.

T F 16. When you play golf, take note of how your foursome is keeping its place on the course. If your group is playing slowly and not keeping its place on the course, you should either urge your group to catch up and maintain its position, or have your group invite the following foursome to play through.

T F 17. Be careful where you stand on the putting green. Do not stand in anyone's line of putt—either in back of the ball or beyond the cup. Also, be certain that your shadow is not cast in the line of play.

T F 18. Chances are that divots dug from the fairway will not grow back, so do not bother to replace them.

T F 19. To hit a good iron shot you must take a divot. So, when you take a practice swing with an iron make sure you take a divot.

T F 20. If you hit your ball into the wrong fairway, you do not have the right-of-way. Before entering that fairway, be certain it is safe to do so, and, be sure you do not bother golfers playing down that fairway.

T F 21. Watch the shot results of the players in your group, so if necessary, you can help in the search for a ball.

T F 22. If a player in your group is having trouble with his game, watch his swing and volunteer some tips to help him improve his strokes.

T F 23. If your ball comes to rest on the wrong putting green, lift the ball from that green. Drop the ball well off the green and not nearer the hole you are playing. There is no penalty.

T F 24. When you enter a sand trap to play a shot, enter at the lowest bank and take the shortest route to the ball.

T F 25. After all players of your foursome hole out, and before you leave the putting green, be certain to check the accuracy of all scores for the hole just played.

T F 26. It is all right to leave your golf bag (or golf bag and cart) at the front of the green, if you hurry to move the golf bag when you have completed play on the green.

T F 27. To speed up play on the course, it is all right to shoot toward the putting green as soon as the players in front have replaced the flagstick in the hole.

T F 28. If you are not putting well, try a few practice putts after your group completes play on each green.

T F 29. When you hold the flagstick for a player, hold both the stick and the banner with the stick remaining in the cup. Stand to one side of the hole and be certain that your shadow is not cast across the player's line of putt.

T F 30. When your group has finished playing a hole, replace the flagstick and leave the green immediately. Do not stand on the green to review play of the hole or to mark your scores on the score card.

T F 31. When your group has been extended the courtesy of playing through another group, you should express your appreciation and proceed with your play without delay.

T F   32. As soon as you hole out your putt, you should remove the ball from the cup.

T F   33. If you hit a ball that is travelling toward someone and may endanger that person, call "FORE!" loudly. At your earliest convenience, express your apology to that person.

T F   34. If players ahead are playing slowly and holding up play, you may prompt them to speed up their play by hitting your shots toward them when you judge they are just moving out of range.

T F   35. Three practices to adopt for care of the putting green are: walk carefully on the green, do not step or stand at the edge of the cup, and repair ball marks on the green.

T F   36. If you tee off first and your drive goes way off line into the wrong fairway or rough, to speed up play, pick up your clubs and hurry to your shot while the other players of your group are teeing off.

T F   37. One player in your foursome is especially deliberate in his preparation for each shot, thus taking a lot of time. There is apparently nothing the other players can do, so you and the other players of the group might as well adopt the same, deliberate style of play.

T F   38. If a player is new to the game and is playing his first rounds of golf, his scores for the early rounds are not so important that his scorekeeping and play should merit holding up the game of other people on the course.

T F   39. It is good practice to mark and lift your ball before each putt you play on the green.

T F   40. When you remove the flagstick from the hole, lay it on the green out of play. Do not drop or throw the flagstick onto the green.

II. RULES

Section 2, Definitions

T F   41. A player has "addressed the ball" when he has taken his stance and grounded the club, except that in a hazard a player has "addressed the ball" when he has taken his stance.

T F   42. "Through the green" includes all of the course except all hazards and the tee and the putting green of the hole being played.

T F   43. If a ball lies so any part of it is touching the green, the ball is deemed to be on the putting green.

T F   44. If out of bounds is fixed by a line on the ground, the line itself is out of bounds. If out of bounds is fixed by stakes, the out of bounds line is determined by the nearest inside points of the stakes at ground level.

T F   45. Sand and loose soil are loose impediments on the putting green only.

Rule 3

T F   46. A player is allowed to carry a maximum of fourteen clubs to play a round.

T F   47. In a friendly game of golf, borrowing a club from another player is common and accepted practice.

T F   48. The rules state specifically that a player may carry not more than fourteen clubs, consisting of one putter, nine irons, and four woods.

Rule 4

T F   49. Golf rules are too complex to master, so in a friendly game where players are out to have fun, the rules may be changed to suit the players.

T F   50. The penalty for waiving a rule is disqualification.

Rule 5

T F   51. Stroke play. A player stamps down the surface of the green in his line of putt. The penalty is two strokes. (*Also Rule 17*)

T F 52. Stroke play. On the fairway. A player pulls out a dandelion growing back of the ball. The penalty is two strokes. (*Also Rule 17*)

T F 53. Stroke play. Before playing his first shot from the teeing area, a player presses down the grass back of the ball. The penalty is two strokes. (*Also Rule 17 and Definition 5*)

T F 54. The general penalty for breach of a rule in stroke play is one stroke.

T F 55. Match play. Before playing a shot from under a tree, a player breaks a small limb from the tree. The penalty is loss of hole. (*Also Rule 17*)

T F 56. Match play. A player grounds his club in a sand trap. The penalty is one stroke. (*Also Rule 33*)

T F 57. The general penalty for breach of a rule in match play is loss of hole.

Rule 6 (Also Definition 34)

T F 58. The greatest margin by which a player can win an 18-hole match is 10-8.

T F 59. A player can only win an 18-hole match play round by having a lower total 18-hole score than his opponent.

T F 60. Player A is dormie 2. A loses hole #17, so is now dormie one.

T F 61. A match is tied at the end of 18 holes. To determine the winner, players must continue play until one player wins a hole.

T F 62. Player A is dormie 6. "A" wins the next hole, thus winning the match 7-5.

Rule 7 (Also Definition 10)

T F 63. In a stroke play tournament, contestants with whom one plays are called "fellow competitors." In match play competition, the contestant one plays against is called the "opponent."

T F 64. Stroke play. If two or more players are tied for first place at the end of the stipulated rounds, the U.S.G.A. recommends that these players play a round of 18 holes to determine the winner.

Rule 8

T F 65. A practice swing may be taken at any place on the course, provided the player does not violate any rules applying to the area.

T F 66. Match play. During the play of a hole Player A plays a practice shot to the putting green. This player loses the hole immediately.

Rule 9 (Also Definition 2)

T F 67. Match play. Player A asks her opponent, Player B, what club she used for a particular shot. Player B declares that she has won the hole because of the rule violation by A. B is correct.

T F 68. Stroke play. You are allowed to ask your caddie or your fellow competitor for advice.

T F 69. If you are playing a stroke to the putting green and cannot see the flagstick, you are permitted to ask a member of your foursome to stand in and remain standing in the correct line to the hole, until you play your shot.

T F 70. Stroke play. You ask your fellow competitor's caddie for advice. You are penalized two strokes.

Rule 12 (Also Definition 16)

T F 71. A foursome played from the first tee in this order: A, B, C, and D. The scores for the hole were: A-6, B-4, C-5, and D-4. On the second hole the players should tee off in this order: D, B, C, and A.

T F 72. Stroke play. A player fails to play according to honor. The penalty is two strokes and the ball remains in play.

T F 73. Stroke play. A player fails to play according to honor. There is no penalty and the ball remains in play.

T F 74. Match play. You fail to play according to honor. There is no penalty. Your opponent can either: require you to abandon that shot and play another shot; or, allow you to continue play with the original shot.

T F 75. Match play. You fail to play according to honor. The penalty is loss of hole.

Rule 13 (Also Definition 33)

T F 76. The teeing ground, the starting place for a hole, is a rectangular area extending two club lengths back of the tee markers. The front and sides are defined by the outside limits of the markers.

T F 77. The teeing ground is bounded in front by the tee markers and extends back of the markers one club length.

T F 78. Match play. The penalty for teeing and playing a ball from outside the limits of the teeing area is loss of hole.

T F 79. Match play. There is no penalty for teeing the ball outside the teeing area. A player may require his opponent to replay a shot hit from outside the teeing area.

T F 80. Stroke play. The penalty for playing the first stroke from outside the teeing area is two strokes.

T F 81. Stroke play. Player A plays her first stroke from outside the teeing area. She must count that stroke and then shoot stroke #2 from within the teeing area.

Rule 14 (Also Definition 1 and 5)

T F 82. If in addressing the ball on the tee a player accidentally knocks the ball off the tee, the ball may be re-teed without penalty.

T F 83. If in addressing any golf shot the player accidentally moves the ball, the penalty is one stroke.

Rule 17 (Also Definition 17)

T F 84. If a player's ball comes to rest on sandy soil on the fairway, he is allowed to brush aside the sand back of the ball.

Rule 18 (Also Definition 17)

T F 85. The following are some typical loose impediments: stones (not solidly imbedded); fallen twigs, leaves and branches; worms and insects.

T F 86. Loose impediments may be removed from any place on the course.

T F 87. If you move a loose impediment lying within one club length of your ball on the fairway and the ball moves, the penalty is two strokes and the ball must be played as it lies.

T F 88. If you move a loose impediment lying within one club length of your ball lying in the rough and the ball moves, the penalty is one stroke and the ball must be played as it lies.

T F 89. You may not remove loose impediments from hazards.

Rule 20

T F 90. Player A's ball is on the putting green 60 feet from the hole. Player B's ball is lying off the green 50 feet from the hole. The rules state that Player A should play first because his ball is farther from the hole.

T F 91. Stroke play. A competitor plays his approach shot to the putting green out of turn. The penalty is two strokes.

T F 92. Match play. Your ball is farther from the hole than your opponent's ball, however, your opponent plays before you do. You win the hole.

Rule 21 (Also Definition 5)

T F 93. Stroke play. A player plays a wrong ball from a sand trap and then discovers this mistake. There is no penalty. The player proceeds to play the correct ball and does not count the stroke played with the wrong ball.

T F 94. Match play. Your opponent plays the wrong ball from the fairway. You win the hole.

T F 95. Stroke play. You play the wrong ball from the rough onto the fairway and then discover your mistake. You add two penalty strokes to your score for the hole; you do not count the one stroke played with the wrong ball; then you play the correct ball.

Rule 27

T F 96. If you accidentally move your ball in the rough, the penalty is one stroke and you must then play the ball as it lies.

T F 97. Stroke play. Your fellow competitor is helping you search for your ball. He accidentally moves your ball. There is no penalty. You must replace your ball to the spot from which it was moved.

Rule 29 (Also Definition 6 and 21)

T F 98. The penalty for hitting a ball out of bounds or for losing a ball outside of a water hazard is two strokes.

T F 99. A player shoots stroke #1 from the tee. He finds the ball in the trunk of a tree and impossible to play. He may go back to the tee and shoot stroke #3; he may drop a ball within two club lengths of the unplayable position, but not nearer the hole and shoot stroke #3; or, he may drop the ball any distance back of the unplayable position (keeping the spot where the ball originally lay between himself and the hole) and shoot stroke #3.

T F 100. A player hits his third shot from the fairway 200 yards from the hole. The ball travels into the rough and after a search, the player declares the ball lost. He may drop a ball on the fairway at the spot where the ball entered the rough and add one penalty stroke to his score for the hole.

T F 101. You hit your drive from the tee. It is obvious that the ball is out of bounds. You must drive again from the tee, and you are shooting stroke #2.

T F 102. You hit your drive from the tee. You are certain it is out of bounds. You must drive again from the tee, and you are shooting stroke #3.

T F 103. The penalty for hitting a ball out of bounds or losing a ball outside a water hazard is one stroke and the player must play his next shot at the spot from which the original ball was played, (stroke and distance penalty).

T F 104. The player is the sole judge as to when his ball is unplayable.

T F 105. A player may stand out of bounds to play a ball that is in bounds.

T F 106. You are allowed 3 minutes to search for a lost ball.

T F 107. You are allowed 5 minutes to search for a lost ball.

Rule 30 (Also Definition 5)

T F 108. A provisional ball may be played if a ball may be lost outside a water hazard or may be out of bounds.

T F 109. A provisional ball may be played if a player believes a ball may be lost outside a water hazard, may be out of bounds, or may be unplayable.

T F 110. You hit from the tee and you can see your ball is near the out of bounds fence. You hit a provisional ball from the tee. You find your first ball in bounds, so you continue play with the original ball and pick up the provisional ball. There is no penalty.

Rule 31 (Also Definition 20)

T   F   111.   If out of bounds stakes or out of bounds fences interfere with your play of the ball, you may lift the ball and drop it (according to the rules on dropping a ball). There is no penalty.
(*Note: Since the rules regarding dropping the ball may have qualifications, assume in this test that when only the expression "drop the ball" is used that the ball will be dropped according to the rules.*)

T   F   112.   If immovable obstructions such as ball washers, sprinkler heads, benches, or protective screens interfere with your stance or swing, you may lift the ball and drop it without penalty.

T   F   113.   Movable obstructions such as rakes, trash containers, and hoses may always be moved if they interfere with play.

Rule 32 (Also Definition 8 and 13)

T   F   114.   On the fairway or in the rough, your ball lies in casual water, or on ground under repair, or in a runway made by a burrowing animal. If any of these conditions interferes with your stance, you may lift the ball and drop it on ground that avoids these conditions and not nearer to the hole. There is no penalty.

T   F   115.   Your ball comes to rest in casual water in a sand trap. The sand trap is completely filled with water so you can only drop the ball outside of the hazard. You must drop the ball in accordance with the rules and add one penalty stroke to your score for the hole.

T   F   116.   On the putting green casual water is between your ball and the hole. You must either try to putt through the water or putt the ball around the water.

T   F   117.   If casual water on the putting green intervenes between your ball and the hole, you may lift the ball and place it in the nearest position giving you relief but not nearer the hole. There is no penalty.

Rule 33 (Also Definition 14)

T   F   118.   You hit your tee shot into a water hazard. It is impossible to play the ball. You may play another ball from the tee or you may drop a ball any distance back of the hazard, keeping the spot at which the ball last crossed the margin of the water hazard between yourself and the hole. There is a one stroke penalty.

T   F   119.   You hit your ball into a lateral water hazard. It is impossible to play the ball. Your only option is to drop the ball within two club lengths of the margin of either side of the hazard, opposite the point where the ball last crossed the hazard. The penalty is one stroke.

T   F   120.   The penalty for lifting a ball from a water hazard is one stroke. The penalty for losing a ball in a water hazard is two strokes.

T   F   121.   Stroke play. A player accidentally grounds his club in a sand trap. The penalty is one stroke.

T   F   122.   A player purposely grounds his club in a sand trap. The penalty is two strokes.

Rule 34 (Also Definition 12)

T   F   123.   Stroke play. Your ball is three feet off the putting green. You use your putter to stroke the ball and the ball strikes the flagstick. There is no penalty.

T   F   124.   If you stroke your ball from the putting green and the ball strikes the unattended flagstick, the penalty is loss of hole in match play and two strokes in stroke play.

T   F   125.   If you are playing a shot to the putting green and you cannot see the flagstick, you may have the flagstick held up to indicate the position of the hole.

T F 126. When you are playing a putt from the green you should either request that the flagstick be attended or removed from the cup.

Rule 35 (Also Definition 25)

T F 127. A ball lying on the putting green may be lifted and cleaned without penalty.

T F 128. Any sand, loose soil, or loose impediments may be removed from the putting green. If a player moves the ball in moving such impediments, the ball shall be replaced. There is no penalty.

T F 129. Match play. Both balls on putting green. Player A putts and his ball strikes Player B's ball. Player A loses the hole.

T F 130. Stroke play. Balls on putting green. Your fellow competitor putts and his ball strikes and moves your ball. You must replace your ball to its original position. Your fellow competitor must add two strokes to his score for the hole.

T F 131. You may take any type stance you wish to putt the ball.

T F 132. Match play. Both balls on putting green. Player A putts and his ball strikes and knocks B's ball into the hole. Player A loses the hole.

T F 133. Match play. Par 3 hole. Both players have reached the green in one stroke. Player A putts and his ball strikes and knocks Player B's ball into the hole. Player B scores a one on the hole thereby winning the hole.

T F 134. Stroke play. Par 3 hole. Both players have reached the green in one stroke. Player A putts and his ball strikes and knocks B's ball into the hole. Player B must replace his ball, and Player A is penalized two strokes.

T F 135. Match play. Both balls on putting green. Your opponent's ball strikes your ball and moves it farther from the hole. You may replace your ball. Your opponent is not penalized.

T F 136. Stroke play. Balls on putting green. If your fellow competitor considers that your ball may interfere with her stroke, she may request that you either mark or play your ball at your option.

T F 137. Stroke play. You play your first putt and the ball comes to rest 12 inches from the hole. You may either mark your ball or play it.

T F 138. Stroke play. Putting green. If the ball nearer the hole interferes with play of another ball, the U.S.G.A. recommends that the nearer ball be played rather than lifted, unless subsequent play of a fellow competitor is likely to be affected.

T F 139. Match play. You may concede putts to your opponent.

T F 140. Stroke play. Player A's ball lies 4 inches from the cup. Player B's ball lies 3 feet from the hole. According to the rules Player B may concede the 4-inch putt to Player A.

ESSAY QUESTIONS

141.-147. List seven rules of etiquette for play on the putting green.

148.-150. List three rules of etiquette for play from a bunker.

151.-158 List eight rules of etiquette for care of the golf course.

159.-170. List twelve rules of etiquette for playing without delay.

171.-180. List ten rules of safety for practice and play.

181.-200. Define the following terms.

1. Hazards	8. Birdie	15. Grounding the club
2. Honor	9. Eagle	16. Casual water
3. Dormie	10. Fore!	17. Provisional ball
4. Stroke play	11. Addressing the ball	18. Lost ball
5. Match play	12. Loose impediments	19. Through the green
6. Dogleg	13. Stroke and distance rule	20. Out of bounds
7. Obstruction	14. Fellow competitor	

ANSWERS—TRUE-FALSE

1. T	31. T	61. T	91. F	121. F
2. T	32. T	62. T	92. F	122. T
3. F	33. T	63. T	93. T	123. T
4. T	34. F	64. T	94. T	124. T
5. T	35. T	65. T	95. T	125. T
6. F	36. F	66. T	96. T	126. T
7. F	37. F	67. T	97. T	127. T
8. T	38. T	68. F	98. F	128. T
9. F	39. F	69. F	99. T	129. F
10. T	40. T	70. T	100. F	130. T
11. F	41. T	71. F	101. F	131. F
12. F	42. T	72. F	102. T	132. F
13. T	43. T	73. T	103. T	133. T
14. F	44. T	74. T	104. T	134. T
15. F	45. T	75. F	105. T	135. T
16. T	46. T	76. T	106. F	136. T
17. T	47. F	77. F	107. T	137. T
18. F	48. F	78. F	108. T	138. T
19. F	49. F	79. T	109. F	139. T
20. T	50. T	80. F	110. T	140. F
21. T	51. T	81. T	111. F	
22. F	52. T	82. T	112. T	
23. T	53. F	83. F	113. T	
24. T	54. F	84. F	114. T	
25. F	55. T	85. T	115. T	
26. F	56. F	86. F	116. F	
27. F	57. T	87. F	117. T	
28. F	58. T	88. T	118. T	
29. T	59. F	89. T	119. F	
30. T	60. T	90. T	120. F	

Index